" I HOPE YOU DIE OF
CANCER "

MARVIN CLOSE

"I HOPE YOU DIE OF CANCER"

LIFE IN
NON-LEAGUE
FOOTBALL

First published by Pitch Publishing, 2022

Pitch Publishing
A2 Yeoman Gate
Yeoman Way
Worthing
Sussex
BN13 3QZ
www.pitchpublishing.co.uk
info@pitchpublishing.co.uk

ISBN 978-1-80150-048-7

Typesetting and origination by Pitch Publishing
Printed and bound in Great Britain by TJ Books, Padstow

Contents

Author's Note

THIS BOOK was put together from nearly 100 hours of interviews with our footballer. As a writer, I've striven to fact check, corroborate and contextualise, and then added further research to explore and explain the wider world of non-league football, from the thoughts he's shared with me. Between us, we've worked to give as honest a view as we can of what it's like to be a non-league footballer and the world in which they live. It's our hope that you'll constantly hear his voice above anything else that's been added in terms of putting the facts of his life into context.

Introduction

THIS BOOK'S about what life's like for a footballer in non-league, so let's begin at the end. I've been with my current club for 18 months. They play in football's eighth tier, the lowest rung on the ladder I've ever played at and, bless them, the management here still see enough in my 36-year-old legs to have offered me another year's contract. I've happily accepted, because playing here has been a joy. After many years playing as a full-time professional in the top tiers of non-league football, I'm now most definitely a part-time pro. But they've still offered me £300 a week, which is pretty good for this level.

Though you should never say never, I suspect this next season could be my swansong as a player. I still feel fit enough to play, not only at this level but in a couple of tiers above. I may be in my mid-thirties, but I still regularly come top of the bleep tests, beating players half my age. I still rack up regular man-of-the-match performances and try to keep my playing standards high. As I write, Kevin Ellison is still playing at League Two level, aged 42, so if I really wanted to, I know I'm fit enough to push myself on for a few more seasons. But I won't for two reasons.

My first, a match I recently had at Kendal Town's Parklands Road. I'd never played there before during my career and it caused me a great angst and anxiety I'd never experienced before as a footballer. Don't get me wrong you Cumbrians. I've nothing whatever against your esteemed club, but the day filled me with an unexpected dread.

The skies had blackened as we travelled over the Pennines and up towards the Lake District and I wasn't in the most positive of moods. I'd had a bad day: stupid little life stuff, hassle with trying to change my phone provider, an annoying conversation with the bank over a standing order they'd incorrectly charged me for twice. All dull, dumb and dreary but it had put me into a grumpy mood. The rain was pouring down as we arrived and a pre-match limbering-up session on the pitch soon turned into a spot-the-blade-of-grass contest, such was the mud heap we found ourselves skidding around on. I remember thinking that if this match had been in the National's top league, it would have been called off. But it wasn't.

Kendal's a lovely and historic town, the gateway to the Lakes no less. Some of its oldest structures include Kendal Castle and Abbot Hall – and the pokey little knackered corrugated iron-clad stand inside Parklands Road. I know there's little money at this level, but the place was falling to bits. In the dressing room, our toilet wouldn't flush, and the water was turned off. No benches for us to sit on, only a motley collection of highly uncomfortable splintered wooden chairs. It all served to take me into a very dark place. Instead of psyching myself up for the match ahead, all I could think was: *I don't fancy this today. Why am I still playing?*

I remembered running out at Wembley in front of 60,000 in an FA Trophy Final. The big non-league matches I'd regularly been a part of, in front of six, seven, eight thousand fans in good, well-maintained grounds. And here I was about to play on a shit heap of a pitch in front of fewer than 150 shivering souls. The conditions reminded me of matches I'd played as a young kid. But then I was on the way up and ever hopeful, so you didn't care. Here I was at 36, coming full circle and I didn't like it. *Is this what my career's come to?* Call it professional pride or just sheer self-pity but, frankly, I didn't want to be there.

I've never been the most vocal in the dressing room, but I was apparently so quiet and withdrawn before the match that one of our younger players asked me whether I was okay. I said what all footballers reply when they're feeling vulnerable: 'Yeah, no problem.' And I could hear myself echoing it in a more upbeat tone: 'No problem!' Because you never want to show a weakness. That's not part of your job description.

But, unwittingly, he was totally galvanising. His innocent enquiry reminded me why I was there. The senior pro, the captain, the most experienced player at the club. As a role model, I had to set an example. I shook off my low mood and then gave my all in the match itself. I played out of my skin, so yes, I could still turn it on. But as we drove home, I questioned myself again and again. *How many more times can I shake off experiences like this and still care enough about playing?* And each time the answer was frustrating. I didn't know. I really didn't know.

I thought about the options. I knew for definite that I could never allow myself to become an older player who just goes through the motions. I've played with and against enough of those to know what a bad look that is. More importantly, I couldn't live with myself. *So, let's see what the rest of the season brings,* I thought. As we drove, I reflected too on the delayed shock I was suddenly feeling about dropping further down the football pyramid. For most of my playing years, I'd been a much-sought-after full-timer. I spent a lot of my career at non-league's biggest clubs in the National, and then into the National League North, but still being paid as a full-timer. But now?

The level I'm currently playing at is like nothing I've experienced before. There aren't as many members of staff, you wash your own training gear, and the clubs can't afford to lay on food during training, all things I'd been used to for years. Where I am now there are no squad numbers, just 1 to 11, which feels amateurish somehow. In days gone by friends would ask me where I was playing at the weekend and I used to say York or Luton or Stockport, proper big clubs. Now when they ask, I say Corby or Leamington or Kendal. I feel almost embarrassed, like I'm not a proper footballer anymore. Which I know is a terrible thing to say, because it sounds like I'm dissing Corby, Leamington and Kendal, the last thing I want to do. It's not about them, it's about me.

As you drop down through the leagues the money goes down and that has an effect on you too. Not just in terms of sheer economics, but on your morale and self-worth. The players are worse, the grounds are worse and you're distinctly aware that you're part-time. This isn't where you expected to be when your footballing life began at a big professional club. Buddy, you're so on your way down.

What was happening in the world around me was having a massive impact too. Covid had a profound psychological effect on many of us, making us question who we are and what it is we do. Like most of us, I'd hit some dark spots during lockdown, and that put me into a very reflective mood. So, the thought of a swansong began.

And as we drove home, I mulled over packing it in and began to think about the things I'd miss most about playing. The answers surprised me. Very top would be knowing you'll never score a goal again in front of a big crowd. The hairs standing up on the back of your neck when you go to celebrate in front of the fans. I'll never forget scoring in front of my mum and dad, my family, my friends and the supporters, and I'll miss that a huge amount. But, and this may sound strange, I'll miss the training with team-mates more than the matches. That's where the sheer day-to-day joy of being a footballer lies for me and always has. I love the banter and having a laugh as we test one another out, learn how to play better together and try out new ideas. The daft challenges we set one another. Who can hit the crossbar from a standing start 25 yards out, five on the trot? Who can be the first to double nutmeg our big ugly centre-back? The joy of working on new moves and set pieces and getting them right. For years and years, people had paid me money to enjoy myself, doing what I'd always dreamed to do. Yes, I've been involved in spats and fall-outs on the training pitch, but most of the time it's where I've always felt totally at home. My happy place.

We all want to achieve things in life, and I thought about what my legacy might be. I've played over 500 matches, have captained several teams. But my feeling was that I'd retire as a player feeling frustrated for my parents and myself, feeling I should have done better in my career, that I should have played at a higher level. Then I was a little easier on myself. There's only one Maradona, one Messi. From there, only a limited number of players make it into the Premier League, the Championship, Leagues One and Two.

It's all easier to see in hindsight, the mistakes and wrong moves. But the truth is, unless you're a top footballer with a well-paid and dedicated team of people around you, life in non-league can be precarious and lonely. You set out trying to chart a journey forward in your career but unexpected obstacles fall in your way. Injuries that set you back, managers who don't fancy you, transfers you take and instantly regret. And then further down the line and as you progress, that awful moment when the realisation sets in that you're not actually very much in control of your career. At National League level and below, football is a brutal business. Contracts are short, budgets are increasingly tight. Playing in the creative style and the position that I do, I've sometimes become an expendable, a luxury player, particularly at clubs who've decided to play more direct. Can I still say I love playing the game? Sometimes. Sometimes I'm not sure. Now and again it has frustrated the life out of me. We also have to bear in mind that I'm not on a hundred grand a week. Like all non-league footballers, I need to earn a living just to pay the bills.

I'm a creature of habit and I'll miss the wonderfully predictable routine of being a footballer. This is what I've done for many years and it's all I know. As we drove nearer to home, these thoughts, particularly, got me scared. How would I cope with that loss? I've known a lot of players who've suffered mental health problems, alcoholism, you name it, unable to find a new rhythm, routine and motivation to their lives. And this is what I knew I now had to think about seriously. I mean, really seriously.

I remember thinking I won't miss playing in sub-zero temperatures down at Braintree, being marked out of the match by two 6ft 3in midfielders who were kicking me like a rag doll around a rock-hard, icy pitch. I won't miss Kendal. I'll miss being a footballer, and the rest of this book explores why. I may not have hit the heights, but I've managed to earn an honest living playing football for over half of my life. If you'd offered that to me as a kid, I'd have snapped your hand off. I'm proud of what I've achieved.

My second reason for thinking of a swansong is that I want to coach. I want to concentrate on gaining more badges and qualifications. I know the game inside out, certainly at this level, and I pride myself on being articulate and a good communicator. I've picked up a lot of good practice from some really progressive managers and coaches and learned what not to do from some old dinosaurs. I think I could make a difference as a coach. I want to see good, attractive, attacking football on the floor. Could I implement that with a group of young players? We'll see. I've already got my first few levels of coaching qualifications and I'm currently trying to get on the UEFA B coaching course. Hopefully through the Professional Footballers' Association (PFA), but as soon as each course opens, it fills up, which tells me what I already knew. When I do get all my badges, there'll be a legion of ex-players just like me competing like crazy for the limited number of coaching jobs up for grabs.

I always intended to get into coaching and sports teaching and, if anything, I think the pandemic has served to speed up my thinking and resolve with that. I love a challenge, a new project. Now I'm a semi-pro, I have another job. I've trained as a sports teacher and have just started work in a secondary school. It's a different world to anything I've ever been used to and was a total shock to begin with, particularly all the preparation and paperwork. But the job has yanked me out of my comfort zone and I'm learning a lot of new things – particularly how to get ideas across to young people about sport and why it's so important.

Ultimately, I do want to get into coaching at football clubs, although I don't know about managing. I'm not sure I'm the right kind of person for that. I wouldn't mind being an assistant manager, a bridge between the manager and the players. I feel as if I could blow my top if I needed to, but I've seen good ex-players destroyed by becoming managers. I've got so much knowledge to give back and could share all the experiences I've been through. I know what it's like to come through as a young player and how to marshal the mental side of things. I've experienced over 15 years of learning and maturing as a player in the game and it would be a waste not to pass that on.

There's much I want to say about non-league football. For this book, I want to remain anonymous, not just because I'm still playing the game, but obviously I want to coach in it too. As you'll discover, non-league football is quite the closed shop and often a very inward-looking world. I've blotted my copybook enough times as a player and realise how long and vengeful some memories can be to know for my future livelihood that I need to keep my name secret here. Several of the experiences I'm re-telling involve individuals I'm highly critical of. It's important for me to recount these stories because I must give you an honest portrayal of what life's like in non-league. But it would be unfair to name some of these people without giving them the opportunity of a right of reply, as I remain anonymous. As a reader, you can continue to guess who I might be and, if you're a keen non-league football fan, you'll have your own thoughts about the identity of some of the individuals I talk about.

The Beginning

FOR AS long as I can remember, I always wanted to be a professional footballer. My dad was from Salford, that rare beast, a Man United fan who lived locally. Naturally, I followed in my father's footsteps and became a Reds fan too. Like most young footballers of my generation, I grew up wanting to be Paul Scholes, then spent the following couple of decades learning how to be me.

I grew up in a small village in the north of England surrounded by farms and rolling pastures. Depending upon the season, the sharp stink of pig manure or the fuggy, weirdly sweet odour of rapeseed oil. Big starry nights far away from light pollution. My village was a hop, skip and a jump further up the road from the back of beyond. There was one general shop that always had long unsold tins of butter beans at the end of a shelf, a pub, a church and my tiny primary school. It only had 30 kids and the only way we could get a school team together was by joining up with pupils from three other tiny primaries in villages seven or eight miles away. I grew up in a small world, but I was a happy kid.

At home we had a big garden at the back, and I started kicking a full-size football around when I was two. My dad bought goals with metal posts and netting, a proper leather pill and little football boots for me. From being a toddler, he taught me a love for playing football. He taught me how to trap a ball, side-foot, volley on the turn, the whole gamut, and it gave me the greatest joy in my young life. I think that to learn so young that you can be good at something and achieve it is the greatest thing. I got that in spades.

Dad was a really good young player and had been on Oldham Athletic's books. He was offered a professional contract, but my grandfather, who was very strict, persuaded him to turn it down. This was back in the days when footballers' wages still weren't that good. He wanted his son to get a proper job that would last him a lifetime, not a few years. And so he did. He left the promise of full-time football behind him, became a manager in the motor industry, and although he continued to play in Sunday leagues, he passed his dreams on to me.

Every day he'd come home after a full day's work, we'd have tea and then in the spring, summer and most of autumn, Dad and I would spend two or three hours in the garden working on my skills. Sometimes we'd get my older sister to go in goal for crossing and shooting practice, but it was mainly me and my dad. He made me practise skills over and over again, which may sound boring and regimented for a lot of young kids, but from an early age I lapped it up because I could see how I was improving and getting better at the game. And then there was no let-up. When the bad weather began to roll in off the fields and winter set in, Dad and I would move inside to the Kitchen Stadium.

Tables and chairs were pushed against the wall. Plates, mugs and breakables went into drawers and cupboards. Dad would defend the two kitchen cabinets on the one side, while I defended an area around the kitchen door opposite. Inside, we used a sponge ball, but it was the same drill as outside. Dad would teach me how to shield the ball, thread a pass, tackle. He constantly set me challenges. Lob the ball on to the top shelf of the white kitchen cabinet. Head it into the bin. When I was five years old, he challenged me to do 50 keepie uppies. That was achieved and it became 100. Then 500. By the time I was eight, I could do 2,000 keepie uppies at a go.

Some nights the sponge ball would get kicked into the washing-up bowl full of dirty pots from tea and then we'd be pummelling a soaking-wet sponge around the kitchen, sprays of water going everywhere, Mum going nuts. There was no quarter given. I'd shield the ball away from Dad and back hard into him. Toes would be stepped on, tackles would fly in. We'd be screaming and laughing our heads off. One night, our dog ate the sponge ball, but nothing could stop us. We made a new ball out of old newspapers and Sellotape and used that until we could get a proper sponge replacement.

According to writer Malcolm Gladwell, to become expert at anything, whether that be playing a violin or becoming a portrait painter, or in my case playing football, you need to put in approximately 10,000 hours of practice. I reckon I got the first few thousand under my belt by the time I was five, which was also the age I started playing for the nearest town's under-10s as well as my primary school team.

I was gifted technically, but still tiny. My kit was like a dress, it was that big on me. Playing for them, I learned a new skill – how to not get crippled. Playing against nine- and ten-year-olds was an eye-opener. Once I'd dribbled past a player or two or cheekily nutmegged someone, the boots started to fly in. They didn't like being beaten by a little five-year-old twerp one bit, and I soon learned how to hurdle scything tackles and sidestep deliberate leggings over. It toughened me up no end, and although they didn't realise it, the older kids were doing me a real favour.

By the time I was eight, I was playing for the town's under-11s team, which was managed by my dad. From day one he's been the biggest influence on my career, but it's always been tough love. I didn't expect any preferential treatment playing in his team. My dad knew I was good but expected high standards from me as well. If I'd scored a hat-trick, he'd be on my case all the way home in the car. Why didn't you score five? Why did you pull at the shot that went over the bar? You didn't get your body over the ball. Why did you scuff that one at the far post? You toe-poked when you should have side-footed it. Dad would pat me on the back now and again but, knowing football as he did, would never give me false praise. If I was to make anything of myself as a player, I had to dig in harder for him all the time. But it paid off.

I was spotted by a scout from our nearest big club – a League One team with a long history and a well-established centre of excellence. Four of my team-mates and I were asked to go in for a 'trial'. I was the only one chosen to stay and so began a nine-year relationship with my local professional club. It was a big commitment for a kid, two nights a week, but it's all I wanted to do. At that age, if I wasn't playing or practising football, I was watching it live or on TV, and consuming every book and magazine and football programme I could get my hands on.

Some weeks later, I was playing in a small local tournament for my under-11s team and the then-Leeds United goalie Paul Robinson was refereeing each of the short matches. He came up to my dad and me straight after the match to say I'd 'really got something' and he wanted to recommend me to someone at Leeds. Whether or not he did I'll never know, but we didn't hear anything back. The point is, though, I was being spotted more and more.

The centre of excellence was in a large gym next to the ground. Always bloody freezing, with a rock-hard floor. They broke the gym up into different quarters, one for each age group, and worked mainly on skills and tricks and such like. I don't wish to sound cocky, but I already knew them all and was well ahead of most of the kids in the older age groups in terms of technical abilities, let alone my own group. If I wasn't the best player there, I was certainly in the top two or three.

All was going well until the day the centre management decided that, henceforward, we were to play competitive matches against age-group teams from other big professional clubs around the north. This should have been fantastic but it meant we had to commit ourselves exclusively to the club and, therefore, were no longer allowed to play for our Sunday league teams. This was where all my friends were and, when you're just a kid, it's a shock to the system to be pulled out of your social group. It was like having to leave all your mates and go to a new school.

I soon began to loathe the 'competitive matches'. We were ordered to wear suits and ties, loaded on to a coach and then driven to places such as Liverpool, Sunderland and Manchester to play in a match of four 20-minute quarters. You might get one quarter on the pitch, sometimes a quarter plus five or ten minutes. But basically, as a kid, you were driven bloody miles to play 20 minutes or so of football with an ever-changing cast of different players. There was no flow, no coherent play. It was all so bitty and disjointed. The club would say they were teaching us discipline, broadening our horizons and giving us the experience of playing against similar-level talents from further afield. I didn't feel as if I was learning anything and certainly wasn't enjoying it. So, I became a rebel.

I told my dad how much I was hating it and said I wanted to play for my old local team again at the weekends. Dad gave me chapter and verse about what a great opportunity I was throwing away, but in the end he could see how unhappy I was. So back I went to playing on Sundays and was soon seeing all my old mates again and enjoying my football. Even more so when I was selected to be part of a regional team that was to take part in a youth tournament in France. There were young teams from Lyons and Saint-Étienne – and a scout from Manchester United.

He'd heard about me, and told my dad that if I impressed he'd get me a two-week 'trial' at Man United. As Reds fans, you can imagine how thrilled my dad and I were. A fortnight-long chance to show them what I could do at the Theatre of Dreams. Wow. But as the matches got underway, I suddenly felt massive pressure on me, and the nerves kicked in. I didn't play badly, but hardly impressed either. I never got my fortnight in Manchester, and that got me to thinking: *Maybe Dad was right about throwing away an opportunity?*

I decided to swallow my pride and ask the centre of excellence whether they'd take me back. I was under no illusion; they didn't owe me anything. But they did give me a trial, liked the progress I'd been making and took me on again. By the time I was 15, I'd been making such leaps forward that the club signed me up as an apprentice scholar and had me training with the under-18s. And at 15 I also became the youngest player at the club ever to play for the reserve team. The future looked rosy.

But there was no way Mum and Dad would ever let me get carried away. If I ever fell behind with my schoolwork, they were on me like a ton of bricks. Homework was checked up on and had to be done, no argument. I was no 'Brain of Britain' but I was intelligent and, having put the work in, passed all my GCSEs. My parents always wanted me to have an escape route if I didn't make it as a footballer. But hey, why should they worry?

At 17, I was a regular man-of-the-match in the reserves. The local newspapers were giving me purring write-ups, predicting I'd be an important part of the new generation at the club. I had enough money to buy my first car, signed on with my first agent and finished my apprenticeship on a total high. Life for me was looking good. My new agent was utterly convinced the club was going to offer me a professional contract, and although I didn't want to tempt fate, privately so was I. I looked around at the other apprentice midfield players at the club and knew I had more technique and ability than any of them. The only other young player who shared my position on the pitch was a big powerful lad, but he was one-footed and didn't have my ball skills or game understanding.

Come the day of reckoning, I trooped up to the club manager's office, where he and the youth team manager were waiting for me. The latter gave me an encouraging smile and I nodded my head and smiled back. The manager, a hugely experienced guy who'd been in charge at a dozen different clubs up and down the Football League, sat back, looked me in the eyes … and sighed.

'I'm sorry but we're not going to offer you anything.'

I was blindsided. Nine years at the club, and just ten words saw me out of the door. I felt embedded there, a happy part of the furniture, and now in seconds everything had changed. The club manager went on to say he really rated me as a player. If we'd been in the Championship and not

League One, he'd have signed me. As it was, he'd decided to go more physical and direct in the middle, so wanted big, strong players. I was too slight for what he needed, but from everything he'd seen and heard I'd get a contract elsewhere. He was signing up the big powerful lad, not me.

I was totally lost for words. I just wasn't expecting this at all. Neither was my youth team manager, who was clearly stunned. I'd done well at every level I played at and he'd seen me through a lot of it. We exchanged glances, but there wasn't a lot we could say to one another. He looked as crushed as I felt. I rang my dad to give him the bad news and he was really upset. I felt as if the bottom had fallen out of my world. As ever, Dad was straight back into thinking positive. Pick yourself up. You're good enough to find another club. Just continue to apply yourself.

I tried to do that. But as the last couple of months of my apprenticeship wound down, I became a person I didn't much like. Previously, I'd be ecstatic when the first team won. Now, angry and embittered, I'd revel in their defeats. Serves them bloody right. The anger seemed to set me alight on the pitch. I had 11 more matches with the reserves before I quit the club for good – and scored ten goals from midfield. I was playing so well that rumours started going around the club that they were going to reconsider my contract. It wasn't to be.

So, I had to find a new resolve. Thanks to the support of family and friends, I began to lick my wounds and tried to find a new home. I got on to my agent big time and told him I'd go anywhere. I took a five-hour train journey down to South Wales for a trial with Cardiff City while the season was still on. I played okay but nothing special. Pass. Peterborough United called me in, and that was a weird trial indeed – a 60-minute one-off match between 22 players who'd never met before and I was played totally out of position, shielding the defence. I did alright, but nothing outstanding. They too took a pass on me. Now I was starting to sweat. I had no back-up plan. All I ever wanted to do was be a professional footballer and everyone seemed to be giving me the shrug. I wasn't used to this, no way. I'd always been the best in my group, my team, wherever I'd played. It taught me a big lesson, that if you're going to get what you want, you really have to dig in.

I got a call from my agent. A League Two club from the Midlands were showing interest. Apparently, they'd been tracking me for a while and now they knew I'd been released, wanted me to spend two weeks of their pre-season with them. I realised straightaway that this was an opportunity I had to seize with both hands. And head and feet.

It was the toughest fortnight of my young life. Away from home for the first time, I stayed in digs with a really nice, welcoming family, but once in my room I felt anxious and alone. I was 17, not particularly worldly-wise and hardly slept that first night. I had no idea what to expect from my first day at this new club in this strange town. All I knew was that if my hopes and dreams to become a footballer were to progress, I had to dig in. I had to become brave and that wasn't easy. I'd been in a comfort zone at my long-time club, convinced I'd be given a pro contract, and this was all new and frightening. I now had to prove myself to a whole bunch of people who had no clue who I was and had probably never seen me play before. I didn't manage much breakfast on that first day.

I was put through my paces like never before during a gruelling pre-season training campaign. Their manager was a former top international player who proved to be ruthless in getting us fit. Every day for a fortnight we were given 'triple sessions'. First off was a 6am alarm, and then into a local swimming pool for opening time at 7am. A minute late and it was a £50 fine. An intense series of swimming races were next up, and in between each race we had to pull ourselves out of the pool and first do 20 press-ups on the side, another race and then 30 press-ups, another race and 40 press-ups, and so on. If you finished last in any of the races, you had to take part in the very next one. We were absolutely flogged. What made it worse was that although our manager was at least a decade older than us all, he was a superb swimmer and won every race he took part in.

Swimming and press-ups over, it was back to the stadium and a second session of running. An hour and a half of long, laborious, flat-out running. All timed and more fines for those that didn't hit the manager's targets. A welcome break for lunch and then back out to a couple of hours of gruelling football practice – three separate teams trying to variously retain possession or steal possession. Then flipping and flipping back again. I had to think so hard, way beyond the muscle memory.

I'd go home at the end of each day totally exhausted, quickly eat something and then fall asleep. The next day it was more of the same. I'd never been worked so hard in my young footballing life and it was mind-boggling. But as the days passed, I felt less tired and increasingly much fitter. Not just physically, but mentally too. I was being pushed more than ever before and, far from giving in at any point, my growing mental resilience was making me work even harder in the sessions. I worked my bloody socks off, did everything they asked of me and more. I stayed on after training sessions to put in more hours practising my skills. No way was I going to let this opportunity pass me by. I became aware that the manager and the coaching staff were becoming impressed with my work ethic and my commitment. More than anything, I was enjoying my football there and they could see how I might fit into their thoughts. To my relief, they offered me a two-year contract. I'd made it. I was a professional footballer.

It was a team that preferred the ball on the ground and tried to play a passing game. They had me as a starter from the first match of the season and, from early on, I pulled a series of man-of-the-match performances for them. I became a first-team regular and eventually played 40 matches in my first season there. People were really welcoming at the club. I settled in quickly and all was well. Until Christmas.

We had a small squad and a worrying run of injuries came to a head when our prolific goalscoring centre-forward pulled his hamstring. Without him we had few guaranteed goals in the side and drifted slowly but surely into the relegation zone. Life on the pitch got tougher and we couldn't buy a win. Plenty of draws but all the teams around us started on winning runs. At the death we had to win our final match to stay up. True to form we drew 0-0. I was now playing for a non-league club.

Even though we'd dropped out of the Football League and everyone at the club was hurting, I still felt hopeful during that summer off-season. I was still a teenager and had my whole career ahead of me. In a relegation fight, I'd been one of our best players and a regular in the team. I was halfway through a two-year contract and, despite the drop, still on the same money, as clubs hadn't yet started to put relegation clauses into contracts. It was a well-run, proper club. We'd learn from our mistakes, pick ourselves up and bounce right back into League Two, surely?

But we didn't and I'd remain in non-league football for the rest of my career. As each season came and went and each new club came along, I still believed I was good enough to get back into the Football League. But life happened and this is the story of that life. The injuries that came at the wrong times. The clubs I should never have signed for and the managers who were a nightmare to play under. The trials, terrors, pleasures and tribulations of earning a living as a player in non-league football. From clueless coaches to crazy players; cocky referees to diehard fans; bonkers board members to a lazy new generation of footballers. From the endless travel and dark, wet nights to small successes and fleeting moments in the sun. This is my take on non-league football over the past decade or more, its current state and where I see it in the future.

The Pyramid

SO, WHAT is non-league football? I hate the term, because one thing clubs outside of the top four divisions have plenty of is leagues. To call it non-league also seems to suggest it's somehow all amateurish, a much lesser form of football. It could be worse. In Germany, the regional leagues below the top three professional divisions are called *unterklassig* – in English, literally 'underclass'.

Apparently, the non-league description goes back to pre-Premier League days when there were four professional divisions, the Football League. The Premier League was Division One, the Championship was Division Two, and so on. Therefore, all the clubs beneath this were literally non-League with a capital 'L'.

Whatever, our non-league system is something to be proud of. No other country in the world has such an extensive and well-organised pyramid of leagues. It has given me a decent living over the past 15 years or so and allowed me to do what I love most. As a consequence, I've become quite a student of non-league football and its heritage is amazing.

Sheffield FC, still going strong in Northern League Division One East, were the first football club in the world, founded in 1857. Cray Wanderers claim their founding back to 1860, while just south of Sheffield, Worksop Town kicked off as a club in 1861.

If you look through the appendices at the end of the book, you may be amazed at the number of non-league clubs who've been around for the past 150 years plus. That they're still running after all this time says much about the resilience of non-league football in this country. Not all is sweetness and light, but we'll get into that later. For now, let's look at how non-league is organised and what 'non-league' actually means in reality. Bear with me, because it's truly mind-boggling.

Beneath League Two, there are over 140 individual leagues containing more than 480 divisions and approximately 7,000 teams. Bear in mind too that this incredibly extensive pyramid of leagues doesn't even include women's leagues or Sunday football teams. If you're not au fait with men's non-league football and how it operates, this all requires some explaining.

All of these leagues are interconnected, with promotion and relegation at every level. So, in theory, the tiniest of clubs could make their way from the lowliest of leagues up into the Premier. Though this may sound fanciful, although AFC Fylde recently won four promotions between 2007 and 2017 and went from the West Lancashire League to the National League, coming within 90 minutes of making it into Football League Two, losing out to Salford in the play-off final at Wembley. Salford City got there by breezing through four lower leagues and are primed, thanks to lots of mega money, to rise further. But back in the day, neither would have got a sniff at playing in the Football League.

The leagues haven't always been interconnected, because up until 1986 the Football League was virtually a closed shop. There was no relegation and promotion between what's now League Two and the non-leagues. Instead, at the end of a season the bottom Football League club had to apply for re-election by its peers, which most of the time was a complete formality. The old Fourth Division of the Football League (now League Two) was established in 1958. During the following 28 seasons, only five clubs failed to get re-elected by their Football League brothers – Gateshead (1960); Bradford Park Avenue (1970); Barrow (1972); Workington (1977); and finally, Southport (1978).

A lot of non-league fans believed that this was nothing more than professional clubs looking after their own and pressure built to create a fairer system. In 1986, it was agreed to establish an automatic promotion and relegation between the bottom club in the Football League and the top non-league club. The following year, Scarborough became the first team to automatically win a place in the Football League, with Lincoln City the first to be relegated into the non-league ranks.

The National League is now the top tier of non-league – Tier 5 or sometimes referred to as Step 1 – and is largely made up of fully professional clubs. A few promoted clubs retain part-time status until they become more fully established – or get relegated straight back down. Current teams in the National League include former Football League clubs such as Wrexham, Chesterfield, Stockport County and Yeovil Town, and several well-established outfits who have proud histories in non-league, such as part-timers Weymouth, who were founded back in 1890, and FA Cup giant-killers Altrincham, who've knocked out more Football League sides than any other club that's spent all of its history playing in non-league.

The champions win the holy grail – promotion to EFL League Two. The six teams below them compete against one another in play-offs. The winner of those matches earns themselves the second promotion spot into League Two. It says much about the quality of the National League that recently promoted clubs Forest Green Rovers, Salford and Barrow have quickly established themselves in the EFL.

Down at the bottom, four teams are relegated either to the National North or South, depending on the clubs' locations, which is known as Tier 6 – also known as Step 2. Both leagues are a mix of full-time and semi-professional outfits. National League North currently contains no fewer than eight former Football League clubs, including Kidderminster Harriers, York City, Darlington and Chester, plus new boys on the block such as AFC Fylde, and historic clubs such as Blyth Spartans, Kettering Town and Telford. National League South contains notable sides Dulwich Hamlet, St Albans City, Billericay Town, Concord Rangers and Tonbridge Angels.

These two tiers are where I've played most of my football. Beneath them in Tier 7 we have the Northern League, Southern Football League Central, Southern Football League South and the Isthmian League. The Northern Premier currently includes some established old names such as Stafford Rangers and Gainsborough Trinity, plus famously fan-owned new boys FC United of Manchester; the Southern League has former league club Dagenham & Redbridge and old stagers Alvechurch, Hitchin Town and Nuneaton Borough; the Isthmian League has Carshalton Athletic, Corinthian Casuals, Kingstonian and Leatherhead. Where I play now in Tier 8, there are a lot of respected and well-established clubs, such as Marine, Mossley, Leek Town, Daventry, Halesowen Town and Corby Town.

From Tier 8 (Step 4), the leagues become ever more regionalised and local, and although we'll be mentioning a few clubs from these along the way, it's Tiers 5–8 we'll be concentrating on in this book.

As we'll discover later, for the huge majority of clubs playing below Tier 8, the cost of travel is one of their major expenses. Thus, the further down the pyramid you go, the shorter the distances between teams. From Tier 9 down are the regional feeder leagues such as the Nottinghamshire Senior League, Dorset Premier League and the Anglian Combination. Below this are another ten steps, right down to Step 21, where you'll find the Central and South Norfolk Division Five. It's difficult to find a town or large village in England that doesn't have a club representing their local community somewhere on the pyramid.

Just to confuse things a little further, the non-league English football pyramid doesn't only contain clubs from England. We all know about Welsh clubs Cardiff, Swansea and Newport playing in the EFL. But in the National League, there's also, of course, Wrexham, while Merthyr Tydfil ply their trade down in the Southern League Premier Division South. How so? Prior to 1992, there were no professional/semi-professional football leagues in Wales, so the top Welsh clubs were long ago allowed to join English leagues. When the Welsh Premier was started, all the above were invited to join, but declined. Six other Welsh clubs playing in the English non-league – Bangor City, Barry Town, Caernarfon, Colwyn Bay, Newtown and Rhyl – accepted the offer.

Gretna, a small town a mile over the Scottish border, also played in the English non-league for many decades before swapping over into Scotland's leagues, famously reaching the Scottish Premier League before their spectacular crash and burn. Berwick is in England, two and a half miles south of the Scottish border, yet their team, Berwick Rangers, have never played in the English non-league. They turn out in Scotland's fifth tier, the Lowland League, making them one of only a handful of clubs around the world who currently play in another country's football league. For them, once again, it's all about the cost of travel, with Berwick being only a 60-mile drive from Scotland's capital Edinburgh and much nearer than that to many lowland Scottish clubs.

Under British law, the Isle of Man isn't a part of the United Kingdom, but since 2020 the Douglas-based FC Isle of Man have been playing with some distinction in the North West Counties Football League First Division South at Tier 10. Add to that, two clubs from Guernsey and Jersey.

The recent inclusion of the latter has brought some unusual new changes into non-league football. In 2011, Guernsey FC joined the Combined Counties Football League Division One at Tier 10, becoming the first team from the Channel Islands to compete in mainland British football. They were followed eight years later by the Jersey Bulls, who entered the same league. As part of the deal, the Channel Islanders have to pay for other teams' travel to and from their home grounds. Also, most of their league fixtures have to be announced in advance, to allow mainland clubs time to organise their travel arrangements.

* * *

The amazing statistic is that no matter where you live, you're never more than 20 miles away from a football club that's somewhere on the football pyramid. With Britain being the home of football, so much of it is historic. As one town formed its own team, the next town along became determined not to be left out. By the end of the First World War, the majority of non-league clubs we now have had already been founded. Some have gone bust and had to be re-formed, while other new boys on the block such as Whitehawk, Solihull Moors and more recently AFC Fylde, Forest Green Rovers, Sporting Khalsa, FC United and Hashtag United have joined the party along the way. Our non-league system is the envy of the footballing world. So, what's life like inside it?

The Dressing Room

I'M ONE of the lucky ones. Even though most of my career has been in non-league football, for most of that time I've been a full-time professional. When I started to play in the Conference in my late teens, it was a while before I began to fully understand the sacrifices that many part-time players make to turn out in the National leagues and below.

Some clubs I've been at only had a handful of full-time professionals, so could only train two evenings a week between matches. Many guys turned up straight from work, not having eaten, still in office suits or work overalls. If they could turn up at all.

Can you imagine Raheem Sterling ringing up the boss and saying he can't make training because the missus is working nights and he can't get a babysitter? Or that he's been switched to night shifts? Or it's parents' evening at the school where he works? When your main job pays most of the bills, football sometimes has to come second. And if you don't train, you're unlikely to be in the starting XI come Saturday. It's a constant juggle for a lot of players, and sometimes I don't know how they manage it.

Precarious is the word. Players like me are on contracts – a year or two. Sometimes, though not often, three. A lot of part-time players are non-contract, sometimes on as little as 100 quid a week – even at top National level. So if you don't perform well one month, you're out of the door the next. Your best hope is to be picked up by another decent-standard non-league club that's also within easily commutable distance from where you live. Because when it comes to travelling, training twice a week in the evenings costs money and can take up a lot of time.

Even as a full-time player, it can be a schlep. A few years ago, I was signed by a Conference club in the north, near to where I lived at the time. Seemed like a dream move. Decent money, a good former League Two club hoping to bounce back, and just around the corner from my home. But then I discovered I'd been signed as the replacement for an out-and-out winger. This, bearing in mind that I play central midfield, and although I think I have a decent footballing brain, I wouldn't say winger is my dream position.

So there I was, out of position, out on the wing and, not surprisingly, I struggled in my first few matches, got a lot of stick off the crowd and then ultimately my boss. Ended up going out on loan to a much smaller Conference club down in the South East. I'd drive down to evening training sessions and matches and not arrive back home until well after midnight. It was exhausting. For three months I spent more time on the motorway than I did playing football. But at least I was still being paid as a full-time player.

Life in non-league, at every single level, is all about money. Or, more to the point, the lack of. The gap between the Premier League and the clubs I've played for is football's Grand Canyon. It permeates everything, and particularly in facilities. Picture this: Manchester City's £200m City Football Academy is reckoned to be the best in the world. It contains the most cutting-edge sports science, physio and training facilities anywhere. Arsenal's London Colney training ground in leafy Hertfordshire is set over 143 acres and contains ten full-size, expertly manicured football pitches, all with undersoil heating. One of my former Conference clubs trained in a local park, much beloved by dog walkers. There's nothing nicer than throwing in a slide tackle and trailing your body at speed through a freshly squeezed pile of dog crap. Sometimes we'd have to clear the pitch of beer cans, broken bottles and drug paraphernalia. That was, in fairness, the absolute worst of my experiences. But most clubs I've played at, just to find a half-decent all-weather pitch to train on remotely near to your club is a huge challenge.

Obviously, some clubs are better than others in terms of training facilities. I've played at clubs at the top end of non-league who had genuine ambitions to either get into League Two or to return there. The simple truth is, to attract the best players at this level – beyond paying them decent money – the better your training ground arrangements are, the more likely you are to cream off the best of the non-league crop of available players. Let's face it, you don't want your workplace to be a shithole.

One area where a lot of non-league clubs could do a lot more is in the dressing rooms. I've played at a few grounds where it's cold showers all the way. There's nothing more miserable after 90 minutes of trudging up and down a muddy pitch in the pouring January rain than taking a freezing cold shower in a mouldy, smelly shower area. Keeping them clean and well maintained doesn't cost a fortune.

In the National League, your dressing room 'box' is a space that can be the product of feast, famine or just fucked-up clubs. Roughly half of the current National League is made up of former league teams, and many of their dressing rooms are pretty decent. A few short years ago, Yeovil Town were in the Championship and their dressing rooms are neat, tidy, well maintained and what you'd expect from a good professional club. Then there's the rest. I remember playing at Stafford and their away dressing room was a complete dump. Panels on the ceiling all broken or disappeared. Tiles missing from the walls. It stank of neglect. If it wasn't for the fact that you know most non-league clubs have no proper money for improving their grounds, you'd think they kept it that way on purpose.

A few dressing rooms are deeply unpleasant by design. Some clubs deliberately stick the heating on full blast. At one club they had a broken dressing room window that they failed to fix for good reason. Before each match, they'd station a member of their coaching staff outside, who'd quietly listen in to your team talk and then report back to his manager. At another, they painted the away dressing room in dank, dark colours to make it as grim as possible. Whether their manager had some kind of psychology degree, I don't know. But it didn't work.

The biggest cliché in the book was supposedly inspired by Wimbledon's old Crazy Gang back in the 1980s. To wit, breaking into the away dressing room en masse before they arrive, and leaving them little brown presents in the toilets – and elsewhere. If you'll pardon the pun, I've fallen foul of a few Wimbledon tribute acts along the way.

Now and again though, you get to live it large. One of the old Conference clubs I played for made it to Wembley and, my god, how the other half live. Our dressing room was as large as a good-sized five-a-side court and featured an AstroTurf area for warming up. Each player had his own individual booth with lighting, storage space and iPad holders. A long, long way from Stafford, literally and metaphorically. And no one dared leave presents in their hallowed toilets.

Like any workplace, every dressing room is home to a dizzyingly different set of personalities and characters. I've played alongside men with great emotional intelligence, the witty and thoughtful, the bloody dense and the selfish divas, the bullies and the thugs. Sometimes, in your imagination, you just want to stab some of your team-mates in the head to stop their incessant, inane chitter-chatter, droning on about *Love Island* and how they got their latest STD. It used to wash over me when I was younger. But as I've got into my thirties, I've become more intolerant of team-mates spouting ill-informed shite and the dumb, juvenile things that go on.

Take initiation ceremonies. At one club I was at, kids who'd made it into the seniors for the first time were subject to numerous vile acts. Third-worst was being made to clamber up on to the roof of a pretty rickety old stand and sing a request tune to the rest of the squad stood down on the pitch. Second to worst was being manhandled naked on to the physio's bench and held down while a roaring, baying squad of players rubbed Deep Heat and dubbin into every crack and crevice and everything in between down under.

But by far the worst was an initiation that the other players prepared in advance during the close season. After every training session and friendly they'd dutifully fill several two-litre plastic milk bottles with piss, poo and other bodily secretions. This disgusting mix would be left to mature until the next young player graduated to the senior dressing room. While the poor unsuspecting bugger was taking his first shower, the whole stinking business got poured over his head from above.

I've had my car windscreen completely covered with Vaseline. At one club, a couple of the players would go through your clothes in the dressing room and steal your car keys. Then they'd drive your car into town, miles away and park it up on a side road somewhere. Your job was to find it. Another club I was at had this weird and damned dangerous tradition. After training, everyone would go into the away changing room, all the lights would be turned off, and then in the pitch darkness everyone threw boots at one another. And I mean throw. It was carnage. Metal-studded boots were bouncing off heads and faces, and after five minutes the lights would go back on again and people would have blood all down their faces from head wounds.

You can drill deep into as much psychology as you want, but one single thing is more important in a dressing room than any other. Are you winning? Stats show again and again that if a team can put together one or two wins, they're much more likely to achieve three or four. You're happy when you're winning. And when you're winning, you're happy. Sports psychologists talk a lot about having a 'winning mentality'. But that's only theory and words when you're out there on the pitch. Winning a match feels great, and sets you up for the next one. Winning two together makes everyone feel better, happier about themselves and the faces around them in the dressing room. Three, four, five? You begin to believe in your own invincibility.

If you're on a losing run or relegation-threatened, a dressing room can become fractious, divided and clique-ridden. Fingers get pointed, blame games start and everyone starts to look after themselves when things are going badly.

One Conference club I played for had been bumping along in the bottom places all season, and as winter became spring we were staring relegation in the face. Training sessions became increasingly bad-tempered, until one evening the frustration boiled over completely. We had a German midfielder who was homesick and fratchety at the best of times, and a big lump of a centre-forward who wasn't getting in the team. Tackles flew in during a training match on a 4G, and they flew at each other. Punches were thrown, and then the German lad stormed off in the general direction of the gym. Half a minute later, he returned with a bloody dumb-bell and smashed the centre-forward around the head with it. It was mental. They both got fined two weeks' wages and, soon after, both left the club.

A lot of the dressing rooms I've been a player in have walls plastered with motivational messages. To be honest, I find them pretty puerile and most footballers don't even read them. 'In it together!' 'Don't Leave Anything in the Dressing Room', and the most common … 'There's no "I" in team'. Bollocks to that. Although managers and coaches try to preach the importance of togetherness, team-bonding and being a part of the project, virtually all footballers I know are looking after themselves. And I think this is particularly true in the National leagues. When you're on five or six hundred pounds a week and much less – more, much, much more about what players earn outside of the Football League later – you're constantly worrying about paying your mortgage and the lease on your car, getting the next contract and pretty much surviving as best you can.

With a few exceptions, I've got on okay with most of the players I've turned out with, but there are few I'd call friends. My first instinct is always to try to get on with people I work with, although some of them are nutters, who in some kind of weird non-league trickle-down take too much notice of what far better paid Premier players get up to prank-wise. I've grown weary of rotting fish left under the car bonnet, clothes being cut up and set on fire, and new motors pelted with eggs and flour. The latter is easier to shrug off if you're earning a Premier League salary and can easily afford to get the ruined bodywork fixed. Ex-team-mate pranksters, I've only ever laughed at you because otherwise I'd have cried.

I have to take my hat off, though, for one brilliantly clever and well-executed prank that was played at one of my former clubs on a team-mate who really fancied himself as god's gift to women. It became so complex and involved that the whole operation would have made a great comedy film plot.

God's gift let it be known that he quite fancied the sister of one of our team-mates, which is generally bad news for a start. You don't try to pull family of other players. So one of the other lads thought it was high time he was taught a lesson. He set up a fake social media account bearing the woman's name, and over days and weeks sent god's gift a string of messages telling him how handsome he was and how she fancied him from afar, but that he must keep it secret, otherwise her brother would go off on one.

He sent her 'candid' photos of himself, kept pestering her to meet up somewhere and promised he wouldn't breathe a word. And finally 'she' agreed. Now you've got to bear in mind that several of the other players were in on this and were all sharing a WhatsApp group, pissing themselves over every new exchange of posts between 'the two of them'. Now it was time for phase two of the prank.

He wanted to meet her in a nearby hotel – and obviously not to talk about our chances against Halifax Town the following Saturday. 'She' told him to bring champagne and a huge bouquet of red roses. The following evening, brains in his pants, he drove to the hotel, where a bunch of us were waiting in the car park, secretly filming his every move. God's gift made his way to the hotel room 'she' had given him the number for and opened the door, ready for it. Alas, he wasn't ready for the second bunch of team-mates, who were bouncing up and down on the double bed, hooting with laughter, all filming him on their phones. And that could have been the end of it. But no …

The prank had a phase three. God's gift called everyone a ****, sulked in training and generally tried to live down his embarrassment. A few days passed. Matchday came and went and the next time everyone met up the coaching staff called us in for our regular session, to review and analyse highlights from the match. And yes, that does happen more and more at non-league level. My current club, for example, have a fan who's a really talented techie and gives us the footage for free, bless him.

The first clip showed how Halifax had outmuscled us in midfield early in the match. The second clip was a montage of social media messages from god's gift to his new 'babe' and then clips of him being 'ambushed' at the hotel, outside and inside. He was raving mad! Everyone else was falling about. To be honest, it's one of the best, and funniest, bits of team-bonding I've ever been involved in.

All players are different, and nowhere more than when they're in the dressing room waiting for a match to kick off. Some players withdraw into themselves, become contemplative and just want to stay quiet and unbothered. That would pretty much be me. Others just run off at the gob. Sometimes it's bravado or jitters. Other times, players trying to pump themselves up. We all come into it with very different frames of mind. One team-mate was so nervous and jittery before matches that he'd go off to the toilet to literally make himself sick. Stick his fingers down his throat if needs be, because there's no way he'd walk out of the dressing room unless he'd been able to throw up. But then he'd usually go out to play with great confidence and consistency.

My approach is different still. I have a mass of superstitions that probably border on OCD, to be honest. I always do up my left shin pad before my right. Then socks, then shorts and always shirt last on. But it doesn't even start in the dressing room. If I'd had a certain meal on a Friday night and I'd played well the following day, I'd have an identical tea the next Friday. If we were playing at 3pm on a Saturday, I always had to eat at 11.30am on the dot, no matter what.

Good managers know how their players tick and let them get on with whatever it is they need to prepare for kick-off time. We had one player at a former club who, as soon as the gaffer started his pre-match talk, would stick his headphones on and listen to music. Some younger team-mates would look at this guy in amazement – and then look at the boss, anticipating the biggest bollocking from hell. But it never came. The player in question regularly scored 25 goals a season, whatever club he was at, so the manager just let him get on with it.

The best gaffers I've played for have patiently put up with my moaning. I've always given of my best in training, but I'll moan about it afterwards. Why are we running in April? We've just played 40-odd matches. Why are we doing this? Why aren't we working on team shape? And most of the managers I've worked with have shrugged their shoulders and let me sound off. To be honest, most footballers are moaners and that's a fact. You don't get Positive Petes. Good managers know that, because they've usually been players themselves.

Talking of managers, people often ask me how much difference can a boss's team talk make at half-time? At top non-league level, I'd say not an awful lot. There are, of course, exceptions. One manager I've played for who I rate massively is former Notts Forest star, Gary Mills, and to this day I can't understand why he hasn't managed at a much higher level. He's one guy who's not just technically great, but knows how to put it across with great clarity in a really clever and understandable way. Ironically, one of his most inspiring half-time talks was in a match we lost.

We were up against Luton Town, a former top professional club with a big ground and great support, who were steamrollering the division back into the Football League. We were 2-0 down at half-time, but actually playing really well. Trotting back into the dressing room, I for one was feeling down. We'd had the lion's share of the play against, at that time, far and away the best team in the league, but two unlucky errors had us two down.

Gary Mills lifted us back up again straightaway. First, he talked coolly and calmly to us as a group. Then he went from man to man. You should be so proud of yourselves. You've come here and taken the match to them. Each of you, you've all been better than your immediate opponent. We need to run out for the second half with a smile on our faces, and really go at them again. If we score an early goal, it's all to play for. Then he talked about some slight adjustments in our tactics that could help us generally, discussed some little tweaks with individual players, and it made such clear, good sense. I looked around the dressing room and everyone else had got it too.

We went out for the second half, all cylinders firing, and did indeed pull back an early goal. Then we hit the bar, the post, we were all over them, but just couldn't get that equaliser. But in a funny way, it didn't matter because the way Mills had made us feel as a group, showing he had real faith in us as players and in our understanding of what he was suggesting to change. It had a massive knock-on effect.

He treated us all thoughtfully and with such perception. After that Luton match, we went on a long unbeaten run and confidence grew throughout the squad.

Bullying, macho managers tend to be full of shit and ego at half-time. If you're trotting off the pitch one or two down, you're just readying yourself for the usual effing and blinding, the flying cups and saucers, the threats and the insults. But the thing is, the more you get bawled and shouted at, the more it becomes water off a duck's back. You just close your ears and try not to listen, because you know they'll never say anything that might actually help you to change the match in the second half. It's all about 'them' and their reputation.

One thing that might surprise people is just how technologically savvy a lot of non-league clubs are these days. The club I'm currently with have the best backroom set-up I've ever experienced, and they play in the eighth tier. They have a team of three analysts who are exhaustive in focusing on your performance. They 'clip' matches to show how you perform at specific tasks and areas. For example, they may want you to win the ball higher up the pitch, so the guys put together excerpts of your pressing match thus far. They slo-mo specific moments to show what your movement's like and draw arrows on the screen to reveal where you tend to run when you press in midfield. It can be quite embarrassing sometimes, to watch yourself making bad decisions or letting opponents on to you too easily. But it's incredibly enlightening and I've regularly tweaked the way I play with my current club because of what I've been shown.

On matchdays, we have a big screen in the dressing room and, before the match, there'll be a graphic put on there of the team formation for the day. Then graphics showing where you should be individually positioned for corners, throw-ins and free kicks. We'll come in at half-time and the analysts will already have collected and collated the stats from the first half. They can tell you where the ball's been, your pass completion, where and when you've been in and out of possession, details about runs, attacks and clearances. And crucially, where it is you've been falling down.

We also have a strength and conditioning coach who gives us all individual programmes. Every week I have to send him my Apple watch readings as evidence that I'm sticking to his wishes.

Tactically too, much of non-league football has become increasingly savvy and sophisticated about playing in different formations and changing things as a match progresses. Everyone's happy playing 4-1-3-2 and then changing to a 4-4-2 or whatever the passage of the match requires. As my career's progressed, the coaching standards have soared and there's a lot of attractive, on the deck, passing football being played now. Sure, there's still a fair amount of direct, sometimes kick-and-rush football, but to varying degrees there are in the lower divisions of the Football League too.

Pre-Season

FOR THE fans, a time of fresh hopes and new beginnings. For the player still on contract at his existing club, something not dissimilar. You're excited to see what new players the manager's brought into the club and whether or not there'll be more quality around you. You'll have an eye out, too, for anyone good who might be challenging you for your position. Sometimes you look around in pre-season and think, *Christ, we're going to struggle this year.* One club I'd already been with for a couple of seasons had a big-name ex-player as manager who'd spent the summer doing a lot of TV punditry at the European Championships. He returned late for pre-season training and was soon playing catch-up trying to put a squad together. He was only managing to pick up players that no one else wanted.

Listening to the senior players was frightening. They were convinced we were in for a long hard season of struggle, judging by the crap the boss had brought in. And they weren't wrong. As the season began, and just to worsen the problem, we lost our main goalscorer to a long-term injury and the rest of us couldn't score to save our lives. Plenty of shots either side of the goal or into the stands, precious few on target. We brought in questionable out-of-contract players who hadn't played for months and were in no way match fit. Fine for 60–70 minutes but out of gas into the final quarter. Guess what? We lost countless matches conceding late on. Not surprisingly, we went down. We all saw it as early as the first week of pre-season.

If you're starting out at a new club, which I've done seven times now in non-league, it's a whole different messy ball of emotions. Of course, you're excited and hopeful. Will this be the new club that helps re-spark my career? Maybe the bridge that'll take me back into playing league football again? But you're also full of fear and dread. Every new dressing room I've walked into, I've felt nervous. Are the others going to rate me as a player? Who are the lads who also play in my position and are they going to hate me? At one club, a new colleague took me to one side, said he knew how much I was earning and that he wasn't happy about it. The guy told me he was a much better player than me (he wasn't!) and would make sure I didn't get an easy ride in the dressing room. I remember driving home and worrying whether I'd made the right decision. Is this new club going to be a lot of hard work and hassle – even before I step on to the pitch?

Do other players feel this way? I can only imagine so, because I've never asked anyone. That would show vulnerability right from the off, and although I wish it wasn't, the non-league football world I've known for the last decade and a half is a very macho place to earn your living.

All of those fears were made worse in pre-season at all my early clubs, because back then you wouldn't see a football for the first two weeks or so. It was all running and fitness work. So, none of your new team-mates saw what you could do with a ball. It was running, more running and then, just for good measure, some more running. Real old-school thinking, and you'd see more of the local parks and countryside than the training pitch.

If you were kicking off somewhere new, pre-season was also the first chance you had to impress the management and the coaching staff. I always wanted to make sure I'd done everything to get in the starting XI come the first day of the season. And not having a football at your feet for the first fortnight delayed being able to show what you were about. Fortunately, I had another string to my bow.

I've always been fast and, in my mid-thirties, still am. As more non-league clubs started to embrace sports science, bleep tests started to come in – a 20-metre course marked off with cones. Players are lined up, a bleep sounds and you have to run the 20 metres to the other side before the second bleep goes off. Increasingly, the intervals between the bleep times get shorter and shorter and the least fit players begin to drop out. At nearly every club I've been at, it's the goalies that go first. Once they're out, a lot of lazy centre-forwards decide it's okay for them to give it a shrug. This is where I've always come into my own. Everywhere I've played, I've been the last man standing in the bleep tests, always wanted to be seen as fitter than everyone else. I've heard that David Beckham and James Milner did the same, so I've been in good company. If you're at a new club, beat everyone on the bleep tests and suddenly the rest of the squad start taking notice of you.

I've habitually worked really hard to keep fit and well-conditioned during the off-season. Endlessly running up and down hills, getting tailored plans from a personal trainer, doing strength work. But that can backfire. Early in my career, I trained like a madman all summer and then gave it my all in pre-season. I started every match that season up until New Year, then I totally hit the wall. I was really fatigued from months of too much hard training and had no energy. The club was really good with me, altered my training schedule and put me on a different diet. Often, instead of heavy training, I'd go for a swim with the physio. But it took ages to get the proper energy back. For the rest of that season, I mainly came off the bench as a sub. Did I learn the lesson? Probably not. The following summer and pre-season, same again. That's the mentality I've always had. The quickest, the fittest. I'm probably a bit compulsive, but it's always the way I've been.

At all of my clubs, some players have waddled back into pre-season training in a shocking state. Younger lads go off to Ibiza and Marbella with their mates and spend the entire summer partying, pigging out and getting pissed. No fitness training at all, and then the bleep tests start and they're dropping out before the goalies. Management would be fuming at the state these guys were in because often that lack of fitness would see them getting pulls and strains in pre-season friendlies and they'd be out injured for the start of the campaign. Then you'd get older, more experienced players who'd maybe come to your club from a league side and thought they could just cruise because they'd come down a level or two. Pre-season would give them one hell of a wake-up call too.

Part of me would be pissed off with them all for being so complacent and unprofessional. But if they were fellow midfielders, I'd think, well more fool you. I'll be wearing the shirt in front of them come the season's start. All every individual player wants is to start every match. If the other guys in my position are dumb enough to blow up like Ricky Hatton, their problem not mine.

Sports science methods in non-league football have become far more sophisticated. Players are given dietary and training plans to follow over the summer, so there's less of a hiding place. But sports science only works if you apply it correctly. When it first hit the non-league game, quite a few of the coaches had athletic and physical training backgrounds, not football-based, and that sometimes led to problems. You'd get over-trained in pre-season, and at the end of every day your muscles would be that sore that you'd struggle to walk.

Equally, good sports science involves a lot of wise psychology. One southern-based Conference club I played for had a manager who established a 'name, shame and blame' policy for guys who came back off a summer overweight. He'd pin a huge graph on the dressing room wall that was divided into green, amber and red sections. Depending on how your BMI body fat test came out, your name was written up on the graph. If a player found himself in the red section, the manager would place him in the 'Fat Club'.

At most of my clubs, pre-season training involved pretty arduous double sessions – one in the morning, one in the early afternoon. At this particular outfit, the 'Fat Club' were made to endure a third fat-burning session even later in the day. It was a killer for the poor buggers and did absolutely nothing for team morale. Players started the season fractious and resentful: red zone players towards the manager for so publicly shaming them and murdering them out on the training pitch three times a day; several of the rest of us pissed off that team-mates we needed to rely upon in the long season ahead had allowed themselves to get so out of shape. We were waiting, kicking our heels, as they played catch-up, trying to get themselves properly fit.

I was particularly pissed off that pre-season. During the summer, I'd enjoyed a fantastic trip around the USA and, for once, didn't get much chance to train. Although I didn't go mad on the food or booze, my BMI test put me into the amber section and not too far away from the dreaded red.

And yet, once again, I won every single bleep test the squad were given and showed myself to be the fittest player there. I'm fairly slight size-wise, so it only took a few pounds of weight gain to push my BMI score up. As I've said, I pride myself on my fitness, so I wasn't very happy to be publicly seen towards the bottom of the amber section. It just really niggled me. It's little things like this that can fracture team morale early on. I could see what the manager was trying to do, but it was done so ham-fistedly. He managed to create a distracted, divided squad before we'd even played a match. Needless to say, we had a poor start to that season.

I'll be honest, though; my own biggest pre-season mistake was because of a stupid act of vanity. This'll sound mad, but I've always had a thing about my boots looking too big. I'm only a size 10, which obviously isn't huge, but I'm only 5ft 8in tall. This particular summer I saw a pair of flash new Nike football boots that I really fancied. Instead of buying a size 10, I bought a size 8 and squeezed my feet into them. It was tight as hell and my toes were scrunched right up at the end of the boots. But I soon got used to them and I thought they looked really cool. A lot of my team-mates thought so too. In my defence, most footballers like their boots really tight because they tend to stretch once you start playing in them.

Little did I realise that I was storing up some major problems for myself. Over time, it changed the gait of my running. I started to get cysts on the cartilage around my knees and I had to be sent to a Premier League club to have my feet realigned. They pumped steroids into the cysts, and I was out injured for months. It was absolutely killing me. Ridiculous. I went back to size 10 Adidas again like a shot.

A lot of pre-season friendlies may sometimes look like glorified training workouts just to get match fitness up, but winning – and losing – becomes a habit. Anyone who says that pre-season friendly results don't matter clearly doesn't know football. We all play to win, no matter who the opposition is, and the worst start you can get to a season is from a string of friendly losses. Winning is good for morale, simple as.

Now and again in my career I've played a few that were more like cup matches for me. I was at a non-league club in the Midlands who had a long tradition of playing local Premier and Championship sides in friendlies. We played Wolves, who had Paul Ince, towards the end of his career, bossing midfield. He was absolute class, never gave the ball away and we couldn't get near him. The gulf between us as teams was immense. But I did get a compliment from Glenn Hoddle, who was Wolves boss at the time: 'You played well, son.' I lived off that for months.

We had a friendly against Birmingham City and they thrashed us 7-0. It was humiliating because every single one of their players was supremely comfortable on the ball. For them, it really was a glorified training workout. We trooped off absolutely knackered, after chasing shadows for 90 minutes. We played West Brom, and although he may not be a big-name player, Chris Brunt had the best left foot I've ever seen. At another of my clubs, we played Leeds United and I marvelled at Fabian Delph's technical ability. Perfectly two-footed, incredible poise and movement and fantastic decision-making about where and when to play the ball. Although it was a thrill pitting your wits against the best, it was also an eye-opener. Facing directly up against them, you soon realised why you were playing in non-league football and they were at the top. They were quicker and more decisive with their feet, but even faster in how their brains worked.

Without the straitjacket of a fixture list, and if you have a few free days, pre-season friendlies can be organised quite quickly, which has sometimes thrown up some unusual, almost bizarre match-ups for non-league clubs. Back in 2013, Spain's Real Sociedad were on a friendly tour of England, when their planned match against Tottenham Hotspur U-21s was unexpectedly called off. Frantic phone calls were made to try to line up a replacement, but every club that Real tried already had friendly matches organised. Step forward mighty Histon, who currently play in the Northern Premier League Division One Midlands. The match was agreed over the phone and took place at Histon's Bridge Road ground the following afternoon. Sadly, the match was so hastily arranged that Histon were unable to get enough staff and stewards in to work, and the friendly was forced to go ahead behind closed doors. Histon were given an 8-1 pasting but also a day to remember.

Back in 1996, and perhaps even more surreally, tiny Bamber Bridge, who played in the old Unibond Premier League stepped in at the last minute to take on the Czech Republic. It was just before the 1996 Euros; the Czechs had their opening match against Germany at Old Trafford and were staying at a hotel nearby. A friendly against Preston North End had fallen through, so Bamber Bridge got the call. The Czech side ran out 9-1 winners, but given they got to the 1996 Euros Final, it was hardly an embarrassment.

Another nice little perk is the pre-season 'tour'. The level I've played at, we're not talking Asia or the USA, but I did have a bloody good week in Devon once with one of my sides, playing against small local clubs. It was perpetual sunshine; the beaches were great, and we gave every single team a confidence-building thrashing. It was a good group of players and, by and large, we all got on fairly well. On the last night, our manager said we could go out for a drink. We took him at his word. Many hours later we walked through the town back to our hotel, drunk as skunks, knocking on doors and basically being drunken young prats. One guy thought it would be a laugh to run along the roofs of parked cars. And then instead of knocking on doors, he started rapping hard on people's windows. Bear in mind that this was about three o'clock in the morning and you'll appreciate how chuffed the locals were to have us in town.

Someone tried to pull him away and back to the hotel, so he decided to have one final knock. It was way too hard. He smashed the glass and managed to gash his arm really badly. Someone pulled off their shirt and put a tourniquet on the guy. We fled back to the hotel and tried to sneak back into our rooms. But then the police arrived looking for us. By five o'clock in the morning, the apoplectic hotel manager was trying to throw us all out on to the street. Our team-mate was now in A&E and the manager was hitting heights of fury none of us had ever witnessed before. He agreed to pay for all the damage we'd caused to escape charges and it all got docked from our wages. Our team-mate's self-inflicted arm wound turned out to be so bad that he missed the first few weeks of the season.

Players

OVER THE last few years, non-league has been home to many talents. Some well-known to football devotees, some unsung. Danny Rowe was a phenomenon at AFC Fylde, scoring 155 goals in 241 matches, and as I write is still banging them in at Chesterfield. Kabongo Tshimanga, also now at Chesterfield after an impressive spell at Boreham Wood, is an outstanding talent, scores hatfuls of goals and continues to be linked with clubs in Leagues One and Two. Bruno Andrade, now playing for Stevenage in League Two, was a revelation in his spells at Woking and Boreham Wood, and probably one of the most skilful footballers in non-league in recent times.

But who are my heroes? The non-league footballers I have the most respect for? In my time playing in non-league, I've played against some remarkable players. Not surprisingly, a lot of my picks have also played at higher levels at some point during their careers. And a lot of them are midfielders I've had to match up against over the years. So, in no particular order …

Scott Bevan was a giant in non-league football – in more ways than one. The man is a behemoth at 6ft 7in tall and totally shredded. Throughout my career, I've never seen a goalkeeper train as hard as Scott, the fittest I've played against. His body fat must have been around 4 per cent. For a big man, he was able to get down on to the ground astonishingly quickly and was about as powerful as you can get with anything in the air. You'd stand across from him in the tunnel before a match and think to yourself, *How are we ever going to get anything past that?* He had a kick like a horse, and I wasn't alone in thinking he was too good for the Conference. A brave bloke too. He had a kidney removed after a horrific on-pitch accident and it looked as if he'd never play again. But he fought his way back into the game. A product of Southampton's schoolboy system, he's now retired as a player and working as Birmingham City's under-23s goalkeeping coach. In non-league, the clubs Scott turned out for included Kidderminster Harriers, Woking and Havant & Waterlooville.

David McGurk was Mr Reliable as a centre-back. From the North-East, he started out at Darlington. He was a player dogged by injuries throughout his career, but David kept bouncing back, which I really admired him for. I know what's it like to be out injured for any length of time and it takes a lot of mental strength to keep coming back. Over eight years at York City, he played over 250 matches before moving on to Harrogate in the old Conference North, where he went part-time. That didn't change his commitment to the match one iota, and so well did he play in his single season with Town, Harrogate's supporters voted him their Player of the Year in 2014/15. He read the match so well, so it was no surprise to me that he went into coaching and management at Hyde United after he finished playing.

Nathan Stainton is the epitome of non-league spirit. He's never played full-time, holding down a job as a fitness instructor alongside his football career, but Nathan's attitude as a centre-back has always been superb, playing at Boston

United, Gainsborough and Spalding Town. He's a great organiser, good with young players around him and a never-say-die defender. I think Nathan would be the first to admit he's not great with his feet, but he's unreal in the air – a great defensive header of a ball.

A player I really looked up to was Jeff Kenna. Jeff came to non-league late in his career, after an illustrious career in the Premier League with Blackburn, Southampton and Birmingham City, plus 27 caps for the Republic of Ireland. He spent a couple of years in the old Conference with Kidderminster Harriers and what a signing they got. Some former top players come down to non-league and struggle to stay motivated. Not Jeff Kenna. He was always full of effort and energy and kept himself as fit as a butcher's dog. You'd tap one past him, run on and think you had him beat. But a second later, he'd be at you again. Totally relentless, Jeff was the consummate professional, knew football inside out and taught both team-mates and opponents a ton of lessons about how to read the game.

Shaun Cooper also started his career playing at a much higher level with Bournemouth and Portsmouth, then came down to the Conference with Torquay United. A class act, two-footed and really cool on the ball. The guy always seemed to be without nerves, and no one ever beat him one-on-one. But what I liked the most about him was that his standards never dropped. He carried on plying his trade in the National League and National League South with Sutton United and Poole Town and remained the ultimate pro.

I played against Johnny Mullins many times when he was at Cheltenham and Kidderminster and, although he was small for a centre-back at 5ft 11in, I've never seen a better header of the ball. He leapt like the proverbial salmon, beating strikers much taller than him with unerring regularity. Johnny was a smart bloke too, gaining a degree in Professional Sports Writing and Broadcasting from Staffordshire University.

Another intelligent guy is Ben Purkiss. He came through the Sheffield United youth system but then joined Gainsborough Trinity as a part-timer so that he could pursue a degree in French and Law at Sheffield Uni. Such a clever midfielder, he always seemed to have more time on the ball than everybody else. A really likeable guy, I was so pleased for him that he made it into the EFL, turning out for Oxford, Walsall, Port Vale and Swindon.

Alex Lawless is one of the best I've played against. Never gives the ball away, a slide-rule passer and a great all-rounder. A product of Cardiff City's youth system, Alex has turned out for Ton Pentre in the Welsh Football League and Forest Green Rovers, York City, Luton Town and Ebbsfleet. Always a passionate, full-blooded player, Lawless got himself into unexpected trouble when Luton played his former club York back in 2011. With the Hatters three down at half-time, Lawless was so furious about his and his team's performance that he punched the dressing room wall so hard he broke his hand and couldn't make it out for the second half. Needless to say, Luton weren't too chuffed, particularly as the fracture kept him out for a month. He got a tasty fine for that.

One of my toughest opponents was Emmanuel Panther. 'Manny' played for York City over 100 times, most of those as captain, and then for Kidderminster, and Dagenham & Redbridge. Manny started his career in the Scottish Premier League at St Johnstone and Partick Thistle and that experience of playing at a higher level shone through when he played in the old Conference.

A six-footer who was immensely strong and pacy, to try to battle with him in midfield was hell. As I'm quite slight in build, he used to pull me this way and that with his power. But I've always prided myself on being a thinking player, and when I have to play against bigger, stronger guys, I try to use my nous. I'll hold the ball up in midfield and flick it around the corner to our striker or another midfielder and then run around the other side to pick up a one-two, and you've taken their player out of the game. Basically, you suck them in as they're flying into you. Or if you're feeling really on form, a cheeky little nutmeg.

Robbie Wilmott was the epitome of the 'flying winger' and so hard to play against. Quick, two-footed and hard to read, I was often matched up against him during his spells at Cambridge, Luton and Newport. After a match, I always think hard about what I've learned from an opponent, and it's a measure of how good Robbie was that from him I always learned a lot. His timing was superb and he had this knack of waiting until the last split second before he made a pass, wrong-footing you into the bargain.

One guy I was always in awe of was Iyseden Christie. A force of nature and built like a bull, he's one of the strongest forwards I've ever seen on a non-league pitch. The way he holds off opposing defenders has always been astonishing to watch. A bit in the Emile Heskey mould, he never scored huge numbers of goals, but his sheer hard work and muscle opened up so much space and so many opportunities for his attacking team-mates. He had a few seasons in the EFL with the likes of Mansfield, Kidderminster, Orient and Rochdale, but much of his career was spent in the old Conference and then the National League for over a dozen different clubs. Although in his mid-forties as I write, the last I heard, Iyseden is still playing, for Midlands League

Premier side Coventry Sphinx. Although he may never have been a prolific goalscorer, Iyseden does seem to have a thing about cup matches. Playing for Mansfield Town against Stockport County in a 1997 League Cup first round tie, he scored a hat-trick in four minutes, which to this day remains the record for the fastest League Cup hat-trick. When he played for Halesowen Town in the second qualifying round of the 2014/15 FA Cup, Iyseden scored six times against Ellistown & Ibstock United in a 7-1 win.

James Constable may not be the prettiest player to watch, but the lad is an absolute goal machine with over 200 to his name. Big, quick and powerful, he's part centre-forward, part battering ram and a nightmare to play against if you're a defender.

James started off way back in 2003 at Cirencester Town and is still playing today at Banbury Town, where he's also assistant manager. Along the way he had a few seasons in League One with Walsall, Shrewsbury, Oxford and Kidderminster, but most of his career has been in non-league with Chippenham Town, Oxford, Eastleigh, Poole Town and Hungerford. James has been a big fan favourite wherever he's played, thanks to his totally committed, full-on attitude. Player of the year at several of his clubs, he was also named in the 2010 Conference Premier Team of the Year.

A player I respect a lot for different reasons is Liam Davies, who started out as an apprentice at Grimsby. He came out as English football's highest-profile openly gay player. His team-mates didn't know straight off he was gay but, once he told them, it was never an issue. I remember thinking, though, that it must have taken a lot of bottle to tell his team. It showed a lot of courage. But that was typical of the bloke.

I'm told he used to get a lot of banter in the dressing room from his team-mates, but it was good-natured, never malicious. The lads knew he was happy with the jokes and he'd always give back as good as he got. The older players had a quiet word with him early on and asked whether he was okay with the ribbing, because if not, they'd have a word with the rest of the lads. Liam told them he felt comfortable with it. I'm not sure that can have been totally true, but what seemed clear was that his team-mates wanted to be friendly and supportive and not to make him feel difficult. He was one of their own. He just wanted to be one of the lads and not make a big fuss in the dressing room.

Rightly or wrongly, football dressing rooms have always been the home of cutting, blokeish banter. If you're ginger, you get slaughtered. If you're into death metal, you get slaughtered. Whatever. In a weird way, it's almost like an acceptance thing and I hope that Liam never took it as anything more than 'you're alright, mate. You're one of the team.' But there have to be boundaries, otherwise it's no different than hateful homophobia.

The lads would all close ranks for Liam if any opponents started being clearly offensive towards him. One time they were playing North Ferriby, who had a player who wasn't the brightest and called Liam something disgusting. I don't know exactly what it was, but it really bothered Liam. He reported it to the ref and his team all rallied round him. The player was charged by the FA for that. More recently, and I'll say straightaway, it's a bloody good thing more players have become much more aware of the hurt that racial abuse causes BAME footballers. It's a much bigger issue than 'banter' or 'just having a laugh' and it's down to players to educate themselves more on that.

No discussion of notable non-league players would be complete without an honourable mention for the striker Jefferson Louis. His amazing journey began back in 2002 at Risborough Rangers in the old South Midlands League. From there he moved on to Thame United and then Aylesbury, Oxford United, Forest Green Rovers, Woking, Bristol Rovers, Hemel Hempstead Town, Lewes, Worthing, Stevenage Borough, Eastleigh, Yeading, Havant & Waterlooville, Weymouth, Maidenhead United, Mansfield Town, Wrexham, Crawley Town, Gainsborough Trinity, Weymouth (again), Hayes & Yeading United, Maidenhead United (again), Brackley Town, Lincoln City, Newport County, Brackley Town (again), Hendon, Margate, Lowestoft Town, Wealdstone, Staines Town, Oxford City, Banbury United, Chesham United, Farnborough, Chesham United (again), Hampton & Richmond Borough, St Albans City and Beaconsfield Town. Add to that five loan moves to Woking, Gravesend & Northfleet, Rushden & Diamonds, Darlington and Whitehawk.

Now aged 42, Jefferson is still going strong and, in 2021, made his 46th career move to North Leigh FC in the Southern League Division One Central. Along the way he's scored over 230 goals and won an international cap for Dominica. Amazing guy.

So, these are the non-league players I personally admire but, in truth, there's a lot of unheralded talent in the National leagues. Over my years in the game, I've seen playing, fitness and conditioning standards continually rise, helped by a general improvement in tactics and match planning. A lot of non-league players wouldn't look out of place in League Two and quite a few would shine in League One – and have! There are an amazing number who've also made their way into the Premier League. There's a pretty dazzling list of footballers who started out in non-league and are still currently playing regularly in the top flight.

Michail Antonio spent six years with Isthmian League club Tooting & Mitcham before making his climb up the leagues, first with Sheffield Wednesday and Nottingham Forest in the Championship, before finally making it into the Premier League with West Ham. Since 2015, he's made over 200 appearances for the Irons. Fellow Hammer Jarrod Bowen started his playing career at Conference club Hereford at the tender age of 17. With Hull City and West Ham, he's already played over 70 times in the Premier League at the time of writing.

Former bricklayer Charlie Austin kicked off his career at Wessex League Premier Division's Poole Town and played over 100 times in the top flight with QPR, Southampton and West Bromwich Albion. He's now in the Championship, back with QPR. Newcastle striker Callum Wilson made his first appearances for Kettering Town in the Conference, while his fellow England international Danny Ings turned out for Conference South club Dorchester.

Chris Smalling is now in Italy at AS Roma via playing over 200 Premier League matches for Manchester United and Fulham. An England international with 31 caps, he began his career at Maidstone United. Ashley Barnes kicked off his footballing life at tiny Southern League Paulton Town and has now played nearly 200 times for Burnley in the Premier League. His former Burnley team-mate Andre Gray first featured in the Conference North with AFC Telford United and Hinckley United, going on to play over 150 matches in the top flight for Watford and the Turf Moor outfit. And, of course, we all know about the phenomenon that is Leicester and England striker Jamie Vardy, who started his career at the Northern Premier League's Stocksbridge Park Steels.

Add to that retired talents such as England international and former European Golden Shoe winner Kevin Phillips, who started at tiny Baldock Town in Herefordshire; prolific goalscorer Glenn Murray, an alumnus of Workington Reds; and former Telford United man, Craig Shakespeare, and you get some idea of what a steady stream of talent makes it from non-league to the very top.

If clubs are shrewd, it's these kinds of talents that can keep on giving. Negotiating decent sell-on clauses can sometimes create a future financial lifeline for non-league outfits. Dagenham & Redbridge allegedly banked £1.5m from Dwight Gayle's moves to Peterborough, Crystal Palace and Newcastle, and that's a juicy windfall for a small club. Players have a lot of affection for the clubs they started out at or have a big association with and do what they can to help out in times of need. Kevin Phillips rallied support for his old side Baldock Town during the pandemic and helped raise over £26,000 to keep the club afloat.

But not all is sweetness and light. There are also a handful of players I hate playing against, and not all for positive reasons. As a player, I have a reputation for making things happen and I'm a creator, so some opponents deliberately set out to hurt me early on in a match. The favourite has always been the sharp elbow in the face, to cut you, so you'll need to go off for stitches, hoping that if you do manage to get back on, you'll be meek and mild and not looking for further trouble. Or the crunching follow-through tackle, the philosophy being hit him early and that'll quieten him down for the rest of the match. But that never works. I just get back up again and run it off. I still have stud marks on my thigh from a two-footed tackle three or four years ago. But I accept that goes with the territory.

One thing that doesn't and shouldn't, happened to me in a match against Ebbsfleet. At a throw-in, one of their players ran into me and spat full-on into my face. A big disgusting ball of mucus right into my eyes, my nose and my mouth. I was bloody enraged, even more so because the ref didn't see it. FIFA categorise spitting at an opponent as 'violent behaviour', an instant sending-off, and rightly so. Although this was pre-Covid, there are still plenty of other nasty diseases and infections that are spread by mucus and saliva. It's vile and disgusting, for me the ultimate in disrespect on a football pitch. This particular player wasn't many people's cup of tea in non-league. He fought with his own team-mates on the pitch, was reported to the FA for biting a player, and his career took him to over 20 different clubs, most of which he never played more than ten matches for before moving – or being moved – on.

I've also shared dressing rooms with players I couldn't stand. Like any walk of life or workplace, you'll always bump into someone who just winds you up big time. There's the type of player who 'talks a great game' but hardly ever plays one. Always arrogant, nothing's ever his fault, won't take responsibility for his own actions. We had a player at one of my clubs who was so up himself that he wouldn't warm up with the rest of us. He'd go off somewhere else to totally do his own thing. On the pitch he was bloody infuriating. He'd try to beat five men on his own and totally waste an attack. There would be team-mates getting into brilliant positions and screaming for a pass, but he'd hang on to the ball until he lost it and the whole attack would break down. He had a horrendous attitude.

I've shared dressing rooms with out-and-out bullies, who've deliberately goaded younger and quieter players 'just for a laugh'. Some of the clubs I've been at, the team spirit has been awful because of players like that. Then there have been the little cliques who are endlessly at war with one another, constantly slagging off other team-mates and loudly blaming them for the team's shortcomings. Not only does it make it a horrid workplace to be in, but it divides the team and, in most cases, means you don't do very well on the pitch. Managers must sign players who have the right attitude, because in my experience good team spirit wins you matches. That doesn't mean everyone has to be ally-pally, but that you show one another mutual respect.

Throughout my career, I could count on the fingers of one hand how many of my ex-team-mates are still good mates. The saying is, there are no friends in football, and I think that's largely true. I've moved on to other clubs and it's got back to me that players I thought I got on well with at my old club have been slagging me off. 'Never rated him anyway.'

The culture in most dressing rooms is still one of machismo and bravado, so a lot of players would never dream of discussing their vulnerabilities or what's been keeping them awake at night. A team-mate asks you how you are and you automatically say, 'I'm great, just great.' Even though you might not be at all. You might be dying inside for whatever reasons, but you get so used to the relentless banter and ribbing that you don't want to give anyone ammunition that could be used at some future point. So, you button it and go home and talk to your partner or the friends you can trust. But not every footballer goes home to a partner or has mates they can truly rely on and offload with. It's no wonder a lot of footballers develop mental health problems.

Funnily enough, I've found that less of the case at the truly part-time clubs I've been with. The culture is less intense because you're not in each other's lap all the time, training every day. As a semi-pro you train twice a week in the evenings and see one another on matchdays. In the meantime, everyone's out in the real world, away from the bubble, living their own lives doing other jobs or college courses. It seems to give people more perspective.

For me though, no matter how much I might dislike another player, if he was the best option to pass to, then I'd pass to him. I've always tried to keep my professional standards as high as possible, and so several things drive me insane. Players who don't look after themselves, get unfit and overweight, who get pissed or drugged up the night before matches and come in on matchday looking like shit. My strong belief is that we have short careers and we're incredibly lucky to be paid to play football. It should be treasured.

The players I treasured growing up? As a kid, the posters on my bedroom wall were all of Gary Lineker. What wasn't there to love? He scored goals, and despite massive and constant provocation, never got booked. He seemed bright, intelligent and full of personality. But as I grew into my football career, there was only one hero for me – Paul Scholes.

As I began to understand more about the intricacies my job as a midfielder involved, the more I became aware of his vast range of abilities. Scholes controlled the pace of matches at the highest levels by the speed of his passing. When to hold on to the ball, when to slow it down and when to speed it up again. He was a genius at disorientating the opposition. He had so many tools in his box that opponents never knew what was coming next. His awareness was astonishing, as if he could see everything in pictures up and down the pitch. The kind of vision that as a fellow midfielder you'd kill to possess.

I learned so much from watching old clips of Scholes, like how instead of dribbling he'd take out an opponent by briefly 'loaning' the ball on a short pass, knowing he'd be given it straight back. It would happen so quickly – and so often – that opposing midfielders couldn't live with his superior game intelligence. He seemed to understand angles better than a mathematician, which helps when you're playing alongside some of the best players in Europe, switched on as they were to expect the unexpected from him.

Young Players

IF I had my time again as a young player, one thing I'd have done differently is not try so hard to fit in. I'm naturally a quiet person and sometimes felt a bit intimidated in the dressing room as a youngster. I was so worried about getting stick in the dressing room for being in any way 'different' that, when I look back now, I really regret some of the things I did and said.

My shame goes right back to being an apprentice at my first club. One time, I and some of my team-mates got free tickets to an Elton John stadium gig, and I asked out a girl to come along with me. At the time we had to attend courses at a local college to keep our education up, and she was a fellow student. A lovely person, thoughtful and caring and she really made me laugh, which if it's possible, almost makes what I did even worse. The plan was we'd watch the gig then the two of us would go off for a drink afterwards. She turned up in clothes that I worried my team-mates wouldn't think were 'cool' or trendy enough, so I binned her off. The rest of the players were off to a nightclub, so I joined them and left her to find her own way home. I know, disgraceful. You were in that environment where the girlfriend had to be a trophy girlfriend and you were judged on the women you went out with. I cringe when I think about this. In hindsight, I acted like a horrendous human being. Bumping into her again a few days later at college was excruciating. It was frosty to say the least, and rightly so. I'd been a complete tosser.

As a young player, I enjoyed the status of being a footballer. You think you're the dog's bollocks, playing in front of thousands every week, people coming up to you and asking for autographs. I wasn't earning a fortune, but still got paid a lot more than most of my mates. So, I was generous and often paid for drinks on a night out because I wanted to look after my mates. But I can see that if you looked at that from the outside, it could well look like I was being a Flash Harry.

If we had team nights out, I'd buy a complete new set of designer clothes, because you were literally judged by your team-mates. There would be a secret vote, usually conducted by the captain, and the 'worst dressed' got total stick for the rest of the night – and usually the rest of the following week. If you didn't turn up for the team nights out, you got a fine. Over the years, anything from £50 to £100. Now I'm in my mid-thirties and know my own mind, pubbing and clubbing team nights aren't for me anymore and I regularly just pay the fines beforehand.

Most young players are desperate to fit in and the pressure to conform is massive. If someone buys something new, you buy it. If you can be a trend-setter, you're quids in. My first week's professional wages, I spent £300 on a leather Louis Vuitton wash bag. I know, ridiculous. My dad did his nut when he found out, but the bag got a lot of admiring glances in the dressing room. So, the next week, I spent over £100 on a pair of Prada trousers. Off abroad for a holiday? Let's spend £80 on a pair of Ralph Lauren swim shorts.

I don't see that it's a lot different among young players in non-league today. With phones and new technology, it's probably worse. I probably sound like their dad now, telling them to put money away and save to buy a house, otherwise they'll end their football careers with nothing. I do honestly understand the pressure they're under. Been there, done it. But at non-league level, you need to hang on to as much money as you can from what little you earn.

Two things I do find very different amongst young players today, however, relates to respect and effort. As a young teenager, I grew up through the old apprentice system. We were paid little more than pocket money and had to clean the senior players' boots, clean the dressing rooms and be dogsbodies at the training ground, putting out cones, helping prepare pitches and the like. At the end of a session, the youth team manager would inspect our work and if we hadn't done it to his satisfaction we were made to stay on for a further half hour to improve on our labours. It taught us discipline and I think kept us grounded and made us more resilient. It also taught me about punctuality and preparation. I was in the training ground dressing room folding the first-team kit at 7.30 every morning and learned to take pride in getting it just right.

We wanted to become the first-team players one day, so we had an immediate respect for them. We'd be allowed to play now and again in five-a-side matches with the senior pros, and woe betide you if you made a mistake. They'd be on you like a ton of bricks. But it was good for you. They were doing what we aspired to achieve, and you'd never dream of answering one of the senior players back. We got toughened up early. When you trained with the pros, it was men against boys. As a young kid, your aim was to become one of the men. It's a little different today.

Partly because of health and safety rules and regulations and a change in culture within football, young players aren't asked to do any of the hard labour and cleaning and clearing up we were made to do. And it doesn't help them, no way. All they do is train and play football, which is all you might think a footballer should do. But many of these young players come into the match without any sense of discipline or even a sense of punctuality and simply turning up on time.

As a man in his mid-thirties, I've had to get used to 18-year-olds telling me to 'fuck off' or to 'stop moaning' if I criticise or offer advice. Increasingly over the past few years, I've become aware of a growing sense of entitlement amongst younger players. A mindset that says 'I know it all already' that means they refuse to take criticism. 'I don't care if you've got over 15 years of experience under your belt in these leagues, I'm bloody good and I'll do what I want.' What that means is they keep making the same mistakes over and over again, simply because they won't listen. Some of the young kids who've been at my last couple of clubs have been virtually uncoachable and, as a result, their careers have stalled before they've even begun.

Sadly, a lot of parents are feeding this arrogance. At non-league level, you might have a young lad who's come to you as the best centre-half in the area. But he'll be a small-town kid whose only experience of playing the match is for schools and in local leagues. He hasn't the perspective to look beyond that and realise that he still has a great deal to learn. But when Mum and Dad are telling you you're the best, you'll become a top pro and similar drivel, a lot of young kids come to us with big chips on their shoulders. What did Philip Larkin say about mums and dads?

When I was an apprentice, we'd look at the senior players and try to learn from their work ethic. The extra training they'd put in, the sheer hard yards. And we recognised that that was what you had to do to become a professional. Work bloody hard. I don't often see that sense of resilience in young non-league players today. Are you desperate to make it or not? Or do you want the easiest path ever? You watch them train and warm up and notice the sloppiness. Half-hearted, always taking shortcuts. Rarely these days do I see any young players turning up early for training or staying on later afterwards to practise and hone their own personal skills. If you point any of this out, you're called an old moaner and told to piss off.

I've had young players alongside me who've shown real potential but let themselves down with their sloppiness and lack of discipline. This has been particularly true when scouts from bigger clubs have come to watch them perform. The young kids just don't get it. They try to impress the scouts with dribbles and six stepovers and Hollywood passes and don't understand – even though we older players tell them – that the talent spotters are there to look for very different attributes, because anyone can do 'tricks'.

A good scout will be watching a young player even before the match begins. How does he warm up? Is he showing rigour and dedication or is he being lazy and just half-heartedly kicking the ball about? Forget the stepovers, the scout's looking to see whether you're prepared to sprint 80 yards back to cover your full-back. They want to see how you react to making a mistake. Does your head go down or do you bounce straight back in there? How well do you read the game? Can you see a pass? If you're being provoked, do you keep your head and show discipline? They're looking overall at your attitude and your footballing brain. And if they're not that great, the scouts will take a pass on you.

One young lad came to us on trial, having just been released by Scarborough. He was without a club and desperately needed a new contract somewhere. As his trial was about to start, he suddenly realised he'd forgotten to bring his shin pads. He pulled his boots out and they were filthy dirty, like he couldn't care less. And you wonder why he didn't get the gig? You've got to show you have the right professional attitude.

The worst by far are the under-23s we get on loan from Football League clubs. They're sent out into non-league expressly to gain real, adult, matchday experience, because up until that point they've only been playing against other young kids. A lot swan in like they own the club and are doing us a favour. They don't want to listen to what a 'lower level' player has to say, because they're Championship or League One players. But the thing is, they're not. They're just young lads still with a lot to learn, and a million miles away from their parent club's first team.

In some cases, by the end of their loan periods, the penny has dropped. But most get the shock of their lives playing in the National leagues. As soon as the opposition get wind there's an under-23s loanee in the side, eyes narrow. You can guarantee a full-back will go straight through them in the first couple of minutes just as a welcome, and the following 88 minutes will be a general roughing up. Suddenly, these young players who think so highly of themselves begin to hide. They're no longer asking for the ball, just keeping their heads down. Opposition players are having a field day, getting the ball behind them, turning them around, clattering into big physical challenges all afternoon long. Basically, they're given a right old rattling.

I'm not a fan of the under-23s system. It gives young players a distorted view of what adult football's really about, because they only play other youngsters just like them. They're cosseted for too long. I was thrown into first-team football aged 17 and it toughened me up no end. I see that a few clubs such as Brighton and Southampton have been contracting over-age players coming towards the end of their careers to be 'team leaders' in their under-23 set-ups. Not just to play, but to advise young players on a day-to-day basis about their game, their attitude and the very nuts and bolts of developing as a professional footballer. This kind of mentoring is definitely a step in the right direction, but I think the under-23 system needs a total root and branch shake-up.

Being a young player isn't easy, though. Because you play in front of a crowd every week and 'represent' your club, you're held up as a role model. However, like all young men, they're impressionable, make mistakes and are still trying to find their way in life. That's fine if you're a young bloke who's not particularly in the spotlight. You have one too many, make a fool of yourself or get in a scrap and it's just par for the course. Even at non-league level, you get yourself into trouble and it's all over the media.

At one of my previous clubs, the lads had a players' Christmas do. We were in a relegation battle at the time, so, not very cleverly, they'd decided to have the night out in the club's home town, not away from prying fans' eyes further up the motorway somewhere. They got monumentally pissed and one of the young players got into a fight with a fan who gave them stick for being out on the town when they were in a survival fight. In the end, many punches were thrown and four of my team-mates got themselves arrested. One lad broke his hand and it had to be put in a pot, which put him out of action for weeks. The fighting foursome were suspended by the club, and eventually they were given community service. You can imagine – it was all over the local media, then social media and, ultimately, national newspapers were picking up on it. If it had been four ordinary lads on a night out, it wouldn't have warranted a footnote.

Young non-league players watch the Premier League avidly, and what the stars do and say has a big influence upon them. Increasingly in training I'd see team-mates wearing thin white wristbands, and I wondered what it represented. Some cause or charity? No, it's because Paul Pogba wears one. If Raheem Stirling's got a new goal celebration, then the following week everyone's mimicking it.

A big thing amongst the young players at my last couple of clubs has been 'snus', a legal high, much beloved by numerous Premier League players. We had one lad at my last club who had a family member playing in the top flight, and he picked it up from him. As soon as he told the other young players about it and that it was the latest thing amongst Premier League players, everyone was at it. Even Jamie Vardy mentioned that he used snus in his autobiography.

It's a smokeless tobacco that contains extremely high levels of nicotine and is meant to aid alertness and concentration. Its sale is banned in the UK but it's not illegal to possess or use it, so players buy it online from Scandinavia. It's all over non-league now and some lads are virtually addicted to the stuff. A couple of players I know get through two or three plugs a match and have them hidden down their socks. Apparently, you place it under your top lip and rumours abound that one Premier League heavy user has been treated for gum cancer.

Now and again, team-mates of mine have been suspended and fined for recreational drug use and from other clubs I know of players who have been kicked out of the match for taking banned substances. A mate of mine was at a non-league club where something very weird happened. Out of the blue, an FA drug-testing team turned up at one of their Thursday night training sessions and specifically asked for four players by name. I'd never heard of that happening before. In virtually every other instance I know of, players are randomly selected for testing, but the FA had obviously been tipped off.

One of the players tested negative. A second, who was by all accounts a heavy cannabis user, failed his test and got a fine, a short ban and was forced to undergo a drug education course. But it was the third and fourth players who the FA really threw the book at. They'd been taking fat-burners – 'grenades' – through the spring, so that they could look buff on the beach in Ibiza. But as they knew, these were highly illegal banned substances. The FA hit them with massive fines and banned them for a couple of years, but it was all pretty much hushed up and never really made public. It killed their careers, and the two never played again.

As testing has become ever more sophisticated, young players who try to match the system are just plain dumb because everything has consequences. As I've alluded to, managers talk in detail with other managers when they're thinking about signing a player. If due diligence turns up a few drug test failures or evidence of unruly, bad behaviour, you've compromised your chances of moving on anywhere half-decent. I've actually played for a manager who was a regular cocaine user. He'd be spotted snorting away in the toilets on nights out – even in the toilet on the team bus.

Some people, though, are really clever at playing the system. A goalie at one of my ex-clubs spent every close season in Ibiza getting off his face, but always stopped a set number of weeks before the start of the next season proper, so that whatever he'd been using was out of his system.

But there's the rub. Most young players don't think beyond next week, let alone the future course of their careers. The few that do are the ones who tend to get on in football. And I'll be honest, not many young players I've turned out with over the last five or six years have gone on to bigger or better things. In fact, most of them are now earning pocket money turning out on Sundays for their local Dog and Duck.

The Banter

IF YOU have a good dressing room of players who get on well together, there's nothing better than good banter. You might have had a crap week, but you come in and there are players you know are going to give you a lift. Particularly if most of you have all been at the club together for a while. You've got to know one another and are comfortable together and that makes it easier to have a laugh. There's always been a spring in my step when I've left home knowing I was driving into a training ground full of players I got on with. Who I could lift with a joke or a laugh and them me. That's always been a joy.

When you arrive at a new club, some early banter can help you feel like you're fitting in. If new team-mates stick a few jokes on you, you feel accepted because, believe me, the worst is arriving at a fresh club and everyone's quiet around you. You're already getting paranoid, thinking *What's the agenda here? Have I replaced one of their best mates? Why aren't I getting a welcome?* So that first dig is always good to hear. It may seem weird to people outside of football that someone totally taking the piss out of you could come as such a relief, but that's the nature of it. You suddenly feel like you might belong.

At its very best, banter can be the perfect relief of pressure. Training is often intense and gruelling and you're giving it your all. Full-on hard challenging matches can exhaust you. Having a laugh can be a glorious release. At some of my clubs, there have been genuine characters who've had the dressing room in stitches and made us crack up with their pranking. One of the funniest in non-league for me has been Steven Brogan. He's from Rotherham originally and once took part in an episode of TV's *Come Dine with Me* with the Chuckle Brothers. He was much the funnier of the three. Steve would literally do anything to get a laugh. There was one time we were training on a 3G pitch out in the countryside and he spotted a pile of rabbit poo in one of the corners. He pulled us all together and then picked it up in his hand.

'If you all give me a fiver, I'll eat this.' We couldn't believe it, so we all said 'yes'. So, he set about eating this handful of rabbit crap, the lot. He spent the next ten minutes chucking up and we spent the following hour screaming with laughter – and he never got a single fiver off any of us.

Another time, he came out of the dressing room stark bollock naked and conducted the entire training session as if nothing was out of the ordinary. The brilliant thing was that because everyone knew Steve so well, no one batted an eyelid. It was just par for the course for Steven Brogan.

The thing about Steve was he was never malicious. His banter and humour never hurt anyone. But a good few players I've shared a dressing room with most certainly did. This is where I have big problems with 'banter'. I've seen things that if they happened in any other job would immediately be punished as workplace bullying. Shitting in people's shoes anyone? Cutting up another player's clothes? Vaselining all the windows of a team-mate's new car? Which, if any, of these would you find funny – as the perpetrator or the victim?

At one of my clubs, we signed a League Two player on loan. He was a smashing young lad and a decent performer. On the day of his second or third match with us he came down with food poisoning. Most players, unsurprisingly, would have made themselves unavailable for the match. Not this guy. He braved it out and started the match. Halfway through, he shat himself. Bearing in mind the team were wearing white shorts, it was embarrassingly visible. The away fans particularly had a field day and, annoyingly, so did some of our players on the bench, giggling and sniggering. This guy, who was only here on loan and was trying to play through the pain barrier, didn't get the respect he deserved. The boss subbed him and he went off to the dressing room to shower and suffer in silence. But that wasn't the end of it.

The next time we went into training, someone left a packet of nappies on his spot in the dressing room. He shrugged and tried to laugh it off, but you could tell he was well pissed off and was even more annoyed when another packet of nappies arrived for his next training session. And the one after that and the one after that. The 'joke' was wearing thin for all but the perpetrators. But crucially, the player himself had had more than enough. He cut short his loan period and returned to his parent club. We lost a good player, signed on a temporary at a time when we had a lot of injuries, and all because of 'banter'. Some people don't realise when they've crossed the line and really upset another player. Sadly, some do and continue because they're, quite simply, bullies.

Sometimes it goes so far beyond the pale that it totally crosses the line. We signed a new player who was black, and some brain-dead idiot left a bunch of bananas on his dressing room spot. The player said nothing and dismissively flung the bananas on to the floor. What a wonderful welcome to help your new team-mate feel comfortable and at home. What a vile insult. A few players thought this was funny. It was just a laugh! It's just banter! It was 100 per cent racist crap. Racism or any form of discrimination isn't banter. It's unacceptable and has no part in football.

Why does this kind of thing still happen in football? I think the term is arrested development. When I think about it, most full-time players in non-league have never known a life outside of football – me included – which means spending most of your time in the exclusive company of other men. As I've grown older, I've realised that's not a particularly healthy place to be in terms of how you relate to the wider world. The football culture I've grown up through is a totally macho one, one in which you feel you can't show any weakness or vulnerability, a man's game. Football is a totally competitive environment where everyone is trying to outdo one another. You're taught that winning is everything. You have to be strong and ruthless – even if it's with your own team-mates. I always want to win when I'm on a football pitch, but I'm not interested in being some alpha male in the dressing room.

I've been in dressing rooms where players have 'bantered' me in ways that have really hurt, but you laugh and say nothing because you don't want anyone to see you've been affected. I honestly think that there are so many hidden mental health problems with footballers. Because of the macho culture, players bottle everything up. You daren't talk about how you really feel or problems you might have because you don't want to look vulnerable.

God forbid that you talk to your manager or anyone else at the club if you're feeling really victimised. If you worked for any other company you'd go and have a word with HR. But do that at a football club and you're a snitch.

And the culture is that you don't snitch on your team-mates. A lot of managers and coaches don't like to see weakness in their players, and there are quite a few I've played for who'd have taken any complaints about bullying as over-sensitive whingeing. So, in the dressing room, the victim can never win. Lose your rag and you have no sense of humour.

It's like still being at secondary school, because that's the only other experience of life that most of us have had. People outside of football may just think this is immature and pathetic, and they're probably right. But that's the bubble that football is. Lots of lads who've never really grown up. I wish I knew more women footballers to discover what life is like in their dressing rooms. I suspect it's a lot different and possibly a lot more mutually supportive, but I don't know. That's the thing about bubbles. You spend too long listening to the same voices and don't allow yourself the time to hear about other people's experiences.

Money

ONE QUESTION I'm constantly asked is ... how much does a non-league footballer earn? Bear with me, it's going to take some explaining, because in the National League and the NL North and South, it can be anything from £50 a match to a £4,000-a-week contract. How can that gap be so large? So, let me begin in Tiers 5 and 6.

For starters, the National is such an unlevel playing field for a lot of reasons. Clubs coming out of League Two enjoy a parachute payment – and the National leagues are now full of ex-EFL clubs and players. Each time two are relegated, that's another pair of clubs who instantly have a bigger budget than most others in the National League. They generally also have a bigger, longer-established fan base that generates even more revenue, which means they can afford to pay for the better players in non-league on a full-time professional basis. And those players are attracted to these particular clubs because they often have superior grounds and training facilities. How good your work environment is matters in any industry.

As well as the ex-league clubs, a good few National League sides now increasingly have the backing of wealthy businessmen. Three or four years ago, Eastleigh's chairman Stewart Donald was a most generous benefactor, desperate to get his club into the Football League. His approach was simple – sign the best players from the lower leagues and pay them all wads of dosh. They had one very good ex-league player who, I was told, was on £4,000 a week, and apparently another couple joined them from two league clubs in South Yorkshire on £2,500 a week, plus free flights to and from Sheffield/Doncaster Airport after matches and training so they didn't have to relocate.

By comparison and around the same time, tiny North Ferriby, which is basically a small suburb of Hull, got themselves promoted to the National League. Despite reaching the highest level ever in the club's history, Ferriby still couldn't get more than three or four hundred through the gates to watch their matches. They tried to survive on a weekly player budget of £5,000–£6,000 a week. Eastleigh must have been on ten times that amount of budget, as most of their other players were on weekly wages in four figures. At best, North Ferriby's top earners were on a few hundred a week. Not surprisingly and despite valiant efforts, the small Hull-area club lasted only one season in the National Premier. But money doesn't always buy success. Despite the wedge that Stewart Donald pumped into Eastleigh, they still remain in the National League, no nearer to reaching League Two.

Without mega TV deals and sponsorships – or rich sugar daddies – non-league depends so much on matchday revenue, so the best-supported clubs have a huge advantage. The gap here in the National is vast. In the 2021/22 season, Boreham Wood were averaging approximately 650 fans per match. Wrexham were pulling home crowds of 8,500, so the Welsh club were making roughly 10 or 11 times as much revenue through the gate.

In football, money doesn't talk, it screams. In a nutshell, here's another important financial difference between

League Two and the National League, which impacts upon players' wages. In League Two, clubs currently get £940,000 simply for being a part of it. In the National, clubs get £75,000 each – less than one-twelfth of what their League Two brothers earn. So, it's little surprise that many National League clubs are constantly throwing what dice they can afford to get into the promised land of League Two.

There are a handful of smaller, usually part-time National League clubs too, who are happy to be there and stay there, but don't harbour strong hopes of ever making it up another league. To do so would mean them going totally full-time and taking on big new financial commitments, such as expensive ground improvements to satisfy EFL ground standard rules. The knock-on from that, is that those clubs will never be in a position to sign the better players in non-league, let alone performers from the leagues above.

During my time as a player over the last few years, I've seen more and more non-league clubs become a vehicle or a plaything of the rich – obviously, the Class of '92 Manchester United players teaming up with billionaire Peter Lim to take over at Salford. Lim, incidentally, also owns one of Spain's biggest clubs, Valencia. Back-to-back promotions later, Salford are now in League Two and pushing to get further up the EFL. Eco-millionaire Dale Vince put his hand deep into his pocket for Forest Green Rovers and they too are now holding their own in League Two. Money talks.

We all know Middle Eastern money has been buying out the Premier League and now it's starting to happen in non-league football. Through KEH Sports Ltd, Dr Abdulla Al-Hamaidi is now the owner of Ebbsfleet. It's not done them any harm – he's paid for their new £5m main stand along with an on-site hotel. Wherever they end up in the next few seasons, their fans are enjoying a much-improved ground and facilities that should in future make money for the club.

AFC Fylde's hugely ambitious chairman David Haythornthwaite has built them a swanky new stadium, which includes plush corporate facilities and a large sports bar for the fans. Starting out in 2007, Haythornthwaite felt so confident about getting his club into League Two that he had 2022 inscribed upon the players' shirts – the year he expected AFC Fylde to become a full-time EFL side. Fylde made it into the National, but then fell back. Now they're back in the National League North. But with that amount of backing their time will surely come.

Steel magnate Glenn Tamplin took over Billericay Town in late 2016 when they were in the National League South. His ambition was to get them into the Football League, and it was rumoured that for a couple of seasons he was ploughing £30,000 of his own money into the club every week to pay the stunningly high non-league wages of a clutch of top former Premier League and Championship players such as Paul Konchesky, Jermaine Pennant and Jamie O'Hara, all of whom were coming towards the ends of their careers. Along the way, Tamplin appointed himself manager and set about transforming the club. By summer 2017, their New Lodge ground had been totally redeveloped to hold 5,000 fans. Covered terraces were built at both ends of the stadium, a new stand was erected, and seating extended all around the ground. Tamplin stepped down as owner in 2019, but not before spending an estimated £2m on the club. They currently sit exactly where they were when he took over in National League South but have a bright, shiny new ground and renewed ambitions.

And then there are clubs who soon realise that to go in search of the holy grail can come at a price. A lot of clubs who've reached for the sky have found themselves in a financial mess – right back to Scarborough, who got themselves promoted to League Two and found it impossible to get crowds above 2,000 in an out-on-a-limb coastal town of just 55,000 people. They, of course, went bust and are now a phoenix club in the Northern Premier League Premier Division.

So, there are a lot of reasons why there are such stark differences in what National League players are paid, even within the same league. It's a mish-mash of the full-time highly paid, the more modestly paid professionals, part-timers and young kids coming through who are on not much more than expenses.

Talking money and wages is a no-go area with most players in a non-league dressing room and often for good reason. The very nature of life in the National leagues means some players can be earning five or six times as much as others at the same club. That kind of variable can lead to a lot of anger and envy, particularly when team-mates who are known to be on the best money are going through bad patches or don't seem to be putting in a full shift. So, most players tend to keep what they earn to themselves. There are always jokes and banter about it. In one dressing room, a lad we knew to be on a good whack accidentally dropped his wallet. Everyone threw themselves against the walls, pretending there'd been an earthquake.

I've played for big and smaller National League clubs, so let me take you through my financial journey to give an idea of how different circumstances can dictate how much dosh goes into your pocket as a player. Right back at the start of my career as an academy player at a League One club in the 2000s, I was paid the princely sum of £45 a week in my first year, £55 a week in my second and £90 a week in my third.

One of my most lucrative days as a young player was when I was brought on as a sub for the first team in a League One match and got paid a £600 win bonus.

These days not many National clubs pay actual win bonuses. It's more related to your position in the table. If you're in the top four, say, and you win, you'll get a bonus. If you're down amongst the bottom places or mid-table, you're unlikely to get any win bonuses. I've always argued that you should get them if you're flirting with relegation, because it's another incentive to perform well – not that you should need it. But it would be another carrot.

The most I've ever been paid for appearance money in non-league is £100, and £100 a goal. But a lot of clubs don't pay for goals or appearances. They can't afford to, simple as. If you do well in the cup competitions, it's well worth your while money-wise, particularly if TV is involved. At one of my former clubs, we drew Huddersfield Town in the first round of the FA Cup and, although we lost, I walked away with over £500 in bonuses. For playing in an FA Trophy Final I got a £1,000 appearance fee.

My first club in non-league paid me a basic wage of £500 a week back in 2005. Over the next few seasons with them, my wages went up to £600 a week and then £750 a week. I loved it there, but I was starting to ask myself whether I needed to move on to progress. I'd given them four and a half years of good service and my mind was made up for me when we went into my next contract talks. They were only offering me an extra £50 a week. I was at the peak of my game, had given them great service and 50 quid felt like a slap in the face. So, I moved on, and to bigger money.

The northern club I played for had me on a basic of £900 a week. From there, I was transferred to a Midlands club in the National League, who paid me £1,400 a week – my biggest-ever wage as a player. With bonuses I was on well over £70,000 a year, which was a good whack for a non-league player. But all good things come to an end.

Life in non-league football can be precarious at the best of times, but no two words strike bigger fear in a player's mind than 'new manager'. This particular club took on a fresh boss who also happened to be on the board and was trying to save money. He quickly instituted a new regime of wage cuts and, as one of his best-paid players, my name was high on his list. My agent advised me not to agree to the cut. It would have gone to a tribunal but then it would have got messy.

I agreed that I'd go, but they'd pay me up 40 per cent of my contract, which was 18 months into a two-year deal. That was a real shame. I loved living down in the Midlands and, although I wasn't terrifically pally with a lot of the other players, I so enjoyed being there. It had a big club, ex-league feel to it. We always pulled good crowds – 3,000 was a bad day. It felt like you were at a proper professional club.

I took up a one-year contract at another ex-Football League club on not far off £1,400 a week and as it was in the north, so I could be nearer home and not need to travel as far. So, all in all, I was better off. But then disaster struck. Halfway through the season, I suffered a bad hernia and things became a right old mess. The club didn't offer me a new contract and my agent spent the entire summer struggling to get me in somewhere new. I was 26 years old, had loads of experience, and thought at the time that I was doing well in my career. I still had ambitions to eventually get back into League Two, maybe even League One but, thanks to the hernia problems, National League clubs were backing off.

Right towards the end of July 2012, the agent finally got me an offer at a small Midlands club, and I breathed a sigh of relief. For the first time it would mean dropping down a level to the National North. In truth, I didn't really want to go there, but at the time it was that club or nothing – and it did mean I could remain full-time. It turned out to be a nightmare move, largely because of the thicko manager who ran the show, and more of him later. Six months into my contract I was begging my agent for another move. He managed to get me a two-year contract at another National North club but, crucially, they were a strictly semi-pro outfit. For the first time in my career, I was a semi-professional footballer. It was still a good wage though, £700 a week basic. Half of that was in cash. At the time, our best-paid player was on £1,200 a week, even in National North.

The club had a manager I loved and players I really got on with. Again, it was nearer to my home, so there was much less travelling. And it had an ambitious chairman who was keen for us to climb the leagues. He was full of ideas to generate more money for the club, central of which was to build a hotel at the ground. Unfortunately, the rest of the board didn't share his dreams and blocked the hotel plan. The chairman had had enough and left, which wasn't good news for me. Without a generous chairman, the club soon found itself in the red and several players were asked to take a pay cut. For me that meant a drop from £700 a week down to £500. This time I didn't listen to my agent and took the cut in wages on the chin. Turning down my last pay cut had led to me leaving a club I loved and then having the worst couple of seasons of my entire career at two clubs I quickly grew to hate. I wasn't about to make that mistake again.

I stayed very happily at that club for the next few years on pretty much the same money, until I got into my early thirties. Then, for reasons we'll go into later, my contract wasn't renewed and, once again, I was on the look-out for a new club. But the older you get, the harder that is. Now I'm playing for a club who are in the eighth tier of the pyramid. It's a great little club and as a semi-pro there I'm currently on £300 a week. Here though, I don't get paid over the summer break and had to pay my own petrol money each day during pre-season training and for friendly matches. I can't complain – but I do – because this club have the smallest budget of any I've ever played for.

I've had a few signing-on fees down the years – three of the 'biggest' clubs I played for each gave me a 'relocation package' of £10,000 to go towards rent and living expenses. I know of a goalscorer, a good player, who signed for a new club and he was sitting with the chairman talking wages and money when the chair pulled open a drawer and yanked out a big brown envelope. He handed it to my striker friend and there was £40,000 in cash. 'That's your signing-on fee,' said the chairman. I doubt whether that went through the books but it shows you that genuine goalscorers are gold dust in whatever league they play.

I've never enjoyed the luxury of a sponsored car in non-league football. Apart from the very top, well-off non-league clubs and perhaps the odd team who have deals with car leasing companies, it's pretty rare in non-league football, more's the pity. My match kit and training gear usually get paid for by local businesses that sponsor the club and generous fans will buy you a drink in the club bar most times you're in there. It's with a little envy that I look towards the Premier League, and even the Championship, where players become their own 'brands' and want for nothing. In non-league, perks there are few.

Grounds

OVER 15 years in non-league football, I've played at literally hundreds of different grounds. Some have become real favourites. Others I shiver at the very thought of returning to. Some have been knocked down.

It's an outdated old cliché that non-league grounds are generally rust buckets and mud heaps, although there are one or two complete shitholes, and more of them later. A cursory look at the National leagues offers some idea why. At the start of the 2021/22 season, non-league's top tier, the National League Premier, contained no fewer than 12 former Football League clubs – Dagenham & Redbridge, Chesterfield, Grimsby Town, Halifax Town, Notts County, Wrexham, Stockport County, Yeovil Town, Torquay United, Southend United, Barnet and Aldershot Town. Drop down into the next tier, National North and South, and you'll find Maidstone United, Kidderminster Harriers, York City, Boston United, Chester City, Darlington, Southport and Hereford.

Many of these clubs spent decades in the Football League, and over the years, as the EFL's ground requirements and rules have been ever-tightened, standards are generally high at these grounds. In addition, a good number of ambitious clubs with wealthy owners, such as Eastleigh and Ebbsfleet, have done a lot to upgrade their grounds. Others such as AFC Fylde and Barnet have stylish new-builds.

One thing's for sure, there aren't many boring flatpack arenas in non-league football. Nowhere else in the domestic game will you find such variety and quirkiness. There are some fine examples of 19th- and 20th-century architecture out there. Great Yarmouth Town, who ply their trade down in Eastern Counties League Division One, play at the Wellesley Recreation Ground, which is home to the oldest football grandstand still in use anywhere in the world. Built in 1895, it's now a Grade II listed building. And the ground's next to the beach. Wingate & Finchley's Maurice Rebak Stadium boasts an amazing 1930s Art Deco stand with a curved roof. Stourbridge's War Memorial Ground is shared with the local cricket club. Half of the stadium's playing area is a football pitch. In the off-season, it extends out to become a cricket pitch. So, when Stourbridge are playing football there, they're the only non-league side to have a cricket pavilion at one end.

Did you think that Forest Green Rovers had the only ecologically friendly stadium in the country? Wrong. Dartford FC, currently down in National League South, have an amazing new ground. Wembley and the Emirates are most surely bigger new-build stadiums but, when it comes to green credentials, neither approach Prince's Park. The stadium produces its own electricity from solar panels and is serviced by a water recycling system, with rain being filtered and reused in the toilets. The pitch is two metres below ground level to reduce light and noise pollution, and the stand roofs are covered in vegetation for insulation and to help the ground blend in with its green surroundings.

Some grounds are a joy to visit, simply because of their location. Mossley FC's Seel Park looks out over the Pennine foothills. Windsor FC, who are in the Combined Counties League Premier Division North, play at the 4,500-capacity Stag Meadows in the Queen's Royal Field next to Windsor Castle. And Matlock Town's Causeway Stadium has fantastic views of nearby Riber Castle and the Peak District.

Some have their own quirky peculiarities. Bower Field, home to Stalybridge Celtic since 1909, has an iconic sloping pitch that I know to my cost can become a ski slope in the frost and ice. The Isthmian League's Canvey Island FC is one the few grounds in the UK that's below sea level and is only 50 metres or so from the River Thames. Further along the river is the virtually uninhabited Desborough Island, home to a nature reserve, a water treatment plant and the Elmbridge Sports Hub, the shared home of Southern League Premier Division South rivals, Walton & Hersham and Walton Casuals. The uber-trendy Dulwich Hamlet, whose boisterously committed ultra fans have made them the St Pauli of non-league football, possess a ground that, although nothing fancy, is always bursting with crowd atmosphere.

From a player's point of view, a lot of my favourite grounds in the National leagues belong to former EFL clubs. Generally, it's because their facilities, changing rooms and ambience are those of good, well-run professional clubs. As a player, these are your workplaces, and you want them to be half-decent. There's nothing worse after a match than cold showers in a ground that's falling to bits.

I love Wrexham's Racecourse Ground. The moment you pass through its doors you feel the history of the place. The world's oldest remaining international football stadium, it's also hosted more Wales internationals than any other ground. Wrexham have been there since 1864 and before that it was the site of a cricket ground. The pitch is always in great nick and its fans generate a fantastic atmosphere. A joy of a ground to play at. It's great for supporters – Wrexham's railway station is literally next door – and now of course it has its own touch of Hollywood glamour, thanks to Ryan Reynolds and Rob McElhenney buying out the club.

There are a lot of reasons not to like Grimsby Town's Blundell Park. It's slap bang in the middle of a housing estate and, with it being a stone's throw from the North Sea and its strong winds, whenever I've turned out there it has always been freezing. But I love playing there. It's a proper old-fashioned ground and has some of the most vocal fans in non-league. I've been to a Lincolnshire derby there – Grimsby Town v Lincoln City – and the atmosphere in the ground was buzzing. It has an imposing two-tier stand down one side and because the away end has a low roof it generates a lot of noise. I've heard Grimsby are thinking about building a new stadium further out of town. Needs must I suppose, but Blundell Park will be a big loss to the football world. Of course, as all footballing anoraks know, the ground isn't actually in Grimsby – it's in Cleethorpes.

It's a blast as a player to go to Notts County's Meadow Lane. With a ground capacity of nearly 20,000, it is of course the home of the world's oldest professional football club and a thrill to run out on to the pitch at such a historically important sporting venue. It's still a bit of a head-scratcher to work out how they've ended up in non-league.

Another proper 'old school' football ground I love is Stockport County's Edgeley Park. Even though County are now in the National League, they regularly pull 4,000–5,000 fans to their home matches and the ground has a massive proper Kop-style stand at one end. It's fantastic to play there under the floodlights and always a noisy atmosphere, and not just because of the fans. Manchester Airport is nearby, and Edgeley Park sits immediately under its flight path. Every five minutes or so you hear great roars from the sky, which just adds to the uniqueness of the experience.

Aggborough, home to Kidderminster Harriers, is a great ground to play at. A really well-run club and whenever I've turned out there the dressing room has always been clean and spotless, the staff really helpful and welcoming and it has a great atmosphere on matchdays. As you run out on to the pitch for a match the first thing that comes into view opposite is an impressively big stand.

I loved going to Darlington's old Reynolds Stadium because it was all state-of-the-art mod cons. No expense had been spared on building the ground. But now I have mixed feelings about my past visits there, because of course it was a white elephant – a vanity project for the club's then-owner, the controversial George Reynolds, who nearly destroyed Darlington. Lovely modern facilities, but it was clearly madness. A new 25,000-capacity stadium – the biggest in non-league by far – that struggled to get 2,000 fans in for matches. It all ended in tears with Darlo on the brink of disappearing forever. Thanks again to the endeavour of committed fans, Darlington rose from the ashes and have got themselves back up the leagues to National North, ground-sharing with Darlington Rugby Club at Blackwell Meadows.

It's not just the former Football League clubs who have the best grounds in the National leagues and below. One of my favourite stadiums is non-league's newest – home to FC United of Manchester, Broadhurst Park. I think it's the first English football stadium to be designed, planned, built and funded by its own supporters and testament to what committed fans can do when they get the bit between their teeth. It's a smashing ground to play at. Surrounded on all sides by covered stands, its *pièce de résistance* is a large terrace at the home end, which really adds to the matchday atmosphere. The pitch has always been good when I've played on it and the facilities in general are amongst the best in non-league. The fans sing and chant endlessly.

Telford's New Buck's Head is a cool ground. Whenever I've played there, the pitch has always been in great condition and there's a hotel with a decent gym as part of the stadium. Again, history is important. Telford is a really venerable club and, whenever you play there, there's a real sense that this is an important club, much loved and supported by the local community.

I've also played at some shitholes. I know Barrow have done a lot of work on their ground since returning to league football, but I used to hate going there when they were in the National League. Apologies, but not only is it in the back of beyond but it's bloody depressing. It's in the middle of a grim, grey, post-industrial town that currently has more drug-related deaths per head of population than anywhere else in England. The ground didn't need a museum because it was one. What was worst about it was the dressing room. For starters, it was the size of a matchbox. There was no room for anything and a good few players ended up having to get changed in the middle of the floor. It was always cold, no matter what time of the year. Dull, grey colours, it was horrible, like being in one of those documentaries about the world's worst prisons, being shoehorned into a cell with 15 other guys.

Barnet's Underhill Stadium used to be a real dump. We used to call it the Underconstruction Stadium. It had a weird sloping pitch and about seven or eight separate higgledy-piggledy little stands, some of which looked suspiciously like temporary structures. Happily for Barnet

– and anyone who now plays them – they've moved on to a new ground, The Hive, which is a 100 per cent improvement on Underhill.

No doubt Luton will have done a lot of work on Kenilworth Road since their rise from the National League to the Championship, but I used to hate playing there. The fans were always about to go to war and, unlike a lot of former Football League grounds, the place was dropping to bits and felt like no one cared about it. There was a similar feel to Dagenham & Redbridge's Victoria Road ground. The moment you arrived the first things you noticed were the potholes in the car park and that the stadium seemed to be in the middle of a really rough estate. The pitch was on a bit of a slope, to boot.

A big difference between National League and EFL football grounds came about six or seven years ago. The National League agreed that its member clubs could lay 3G artificial pitches. To date, the EFL are seriously not having it, to the extent that clubs recently promoted into League Two such as Harrogate Town and Sutton United were given a stark choice. Rip up your artificial pitches and replace them with grass or you don't play in the EFL. Both did that, not surprisingly desperate to play at the highest level in their histories. Sutton reckon that it'll cost them £200,000 a season in lost revenue and estrange them from the many clubs and organisations who they rented the pitch out to. I wonder how long it'll be before successful National League clubs who play on artificial pitches 'refuse' promotion to League Two?

On average, a grass surface can only be played on for four to five hours a week before it starts to do real and lasting damage. An artificial pitch can be played on for 50-plus hours a week. The benefits of this to a small club can be massive in several ways. Firstly, they don't need to rent extra training pitches/facilities because they can happily use their own ground throughout the week. A big saving for small clubs. Secondly, it becomes a valuable income stream, as the club can hire it out to local leagues and community organisations, which also further bonds the club with its town. Thirdly, and certainly in the winter months, teams that have artificial pitches have very few matches cancelled because of bad weather. I think it's no coincidence that in Scotland and Wales, where weather conditions are tougher, more and more clubs have gone with artificial pitches. Post-pandemic, a lot more smaller League One and Two clubs will be desperate to generate more money, and I believe there will be more and more pressure put upon the EFL to allow 3G and 4G pitches in their bottom two divisions. And I think it'll happen sooner rather than later.

From a board's point of view, this all makes a lot of sense. From a player's perspective, I have to tell you that playing for 90 minutes on 3G in a full-on match can be knackering. I've heard the argument that a lot of professional clubs have 3G training pitches – so if they have a problem with artificial surfaces, why let their players train on them? Believe me, there's a big difference between playing in a 90-minute match and going through training routines.

It's fine if the pitch has been well watered or rained upon, because the ball glides along consistently on the surface. But if they're dry, the football becomes unpredictable. It skips and bounces weirdly, so you're never sure where or how to spray a longer pass. I find it a lot harder to change direction quickly within a moment in play, because your studs don't get the grip or purchase you get on grass. So, it wrecks your feet and your joints. That particularly poses a re-injury worry, if you've already suffered problems there as I have. I always wake up the day after a match on an artificial pitch aching like hell. But I'm not giving up on 3G pitches.

Technology moves on and today's surfaces are appreciably better than they were a decade ago. The first artificial surfaces were a bloody nightmare to play on. Across Europe, Champions League matches have been played on 3G and FIFA clearly doesn't have a problem with them. So, it may only be a matter of time before artificial pitches become the norm. It's become a very emotive argument within football, though. Many who favour 3G view pro-grass traditionalists as nothing short of dinosaurs, who in turn think the artificial pitch mob are ruining football. I absolutely get how important they are to non-league clubs' financial planning, and how they lead to way fewer match postponements. All I want is artificial pitches that are 100 per cent player-friendly and as good as grass.

Another ground gripe! An atmosphere-downer for me is playing at grounds that have running and cycle tracks around the pitch. We're talking here about the likes of Gateshead, Bradford Park Avenue and Hornchurch, plus a good few others down the pyramid. But here again I realise that it's nearly always a case of needs must. Ground-sharing with other sports makes total economic sense when you're not earning a lot as a football club. Share your costs with other local sports clubs and it benefits everyone. But 99 times out of 100 it spoils the atmosphere for the fans and the players. I remember scoring a goal at Gateshead when a good few hundred fans had travelled away with us, and I could hardly hear them, they were so far away from the pitch. It felt distinctly underwhelming. One of the best things about most non-league grounds is that the fans are generally so close to the field of play. Running tracks seem to suck the atmosphere right out of a ground.

But despite my moans and groans, I've felt privileged to spend most of my working football life playing at grounds that mean so much to their supporters and the histories of their clubs. Like most players, I'm a massive football fan and I totally understand the loyalty people feel towards those little patches of land that house their club. In non-league football, it's the fans that make the clubs – and in a lot of cases, keep them running.

Travel

FOR QUITE a few years, I lived a fair distance from the clubs I played for and never had the benefit of a car share to ease the miles. For two years I travelled to my Southern-based club from the north, which took three and a half hours each way. If I'd been home after a match, I had to get up at 4am to get back down there in time for training. In that two years, I did over 100,000 miles, schlepping up and down the motorway, and I was spending £600 a month on petrol. There would be the odd day when I'd turn up for training after a long early-morning drive and feel knackered before I started. Ah, the loneliness of the long-distance footballer. My next club was only an hour-and-a-half's drive away, but that was still three hours on the road virtually every day to get to training and matches.

Without doubt the driving was tedious and stress-inducing, but it had deeper emotional effects too. Travelling alone so much gave me too much time to dwell on things. Why had I been benched? Why was the manager always on my case? You'd hang on a hurtful remark someone might have made on the spur of the moment in training that day, turn it over and over in your head and make it much bigger than it was. I'd over-think things and take them to heart. *Why is my career treading water? Where's next for me? Am I finished?*

The reality of the non-league footballer is that a lot of travel is inevitable. When you're not earning a fortune and often going from one short contract to another, it's not economic to buy or rent new places everywhere you go. I've slept on floors and sofas, sometimes taken out short lets, but on the whole I'd much rather be home. So, you take the endless travelling on the chin.

Later on, when I started playing for clubs nearer to where I lived, I got involved in more car shares to and from training and the ground on matchday, which was a relief. One car share, there were four of us who'd take it in turn to drive. A trick we used to play was to close the windows tight shut and put the heating on full blast. The first to buckle had to pay for the meal that night. There were always rows over music. When we were in one player's car, he'd blast out really heavy death metal, the last thing you wanted to hear after a match when you were knackered. It used to give me migraines. He got a lot of ribbing from the other lads but, to be fair, he laughed along with us and owned it. With most footballers, it's generally R&B, house and dance music, so he was a real one-off.

It can be good company in a car share when you've won. It's all celebration, everyone on a high, talking through the key moments of the match. But if things aren't going so well, it's a lot different. If you lost and, most importantly, lost badly, you're all trying to change the subject, talking about anything but the match. Because at the forefront of all your minds is that you're going to get a proper hammering from the manager at the next training session and everyone's replaying moments when they cocked-up and anticipating the slagging they'll personally receive. Worst of all for me was if your three team-mates in the car share played and you didn't. They're full of banter about what happened during

107

the match … and you? Well, although you watched it out on the touchline, you're kind of out of the conversation. And the thing about footballers everywhere is that you want to be a part of the team, the action. Not being picked, not coming on, out injured, out of favour – if you're not playing, you really feel it psychologically.

Sometimes car shares can be downright dangerous for your career. Three players I know were car sharing back from a training session. That night their new manager had made his first appearance and they were late getting away. Keen to get home, they sped off from the ground and out on to the country roads but soon got caught behind a little red car that wasn't travelling overly fast. With nowhere safe to overtake, the lads got stuck behind the slow-mover for half an hour. When they eventually got to a stretch of motorway, they raced past the little red car, flicking the 'Vs' and swearing out of the passenger windows. And then for the guy in the passenger seat, the penny suddenly dropped. The driver of the car was their new manager. Terrified that he'd identified them as three of his own players, the lads went in on the next matchday bricking themselves but, as they'd all been picked, thought they'd got away with it. The manager said nothing. They played the match, went towards the car park to leave, and there was the new manager. 'Who,' he asked, 'owns the Renault Megane?' Those three players found themselves sitting on the bench for the rest of the season.

By far the worst, most depressing journeys are the ones to a match you know you won't be playing in because you've been ordered to sit in the stands. That's happened at a couple of clubs where I've been so out of favour with a manager that he's not even put me on the bench. But like the true sadists several managers are, you still get ordered to travel to the match, do some meaningless warm-up exercises on the pitch with the playing squad and then scuttle up into the stands with your tail between your legs. I'm sure it's nothing but a power thing.

At one club, I'd spent weeks being forced to sit in the stand and I was well pissed off. So, to raise my morale, I decided to take my partner for a short break abroad between matches. We had a match on a Tuesday night at FC United, so my partner and I went to Bruges after the Saturday match for a few days. The plan was we'd get back Tuesday during the day and drive over by our own steam to Manchester, where I fully expected to be sitting in the stands again. Bruges, of course, is famous for its beer, frites and chocolate and I had plenty of all three, particularly the strong ales. Basically, I was pissed for three days and when we arrived back in Britain on the Tuesday I had a raging hangover. I got myself over to Manchester, feeling knackered, to the extremely unexpected news that I was starting the match. I was shattered and still the worse for wear, but I didn't dare tell anyone where I'd been and what I'd been doing, let alone how I was feeling. Ironically, I had quite a good match. However, as though I needed one, it was yet another reminder to always expect the unexpected in football.

For Premier League players, the sky's the limit. If London clubs are playing up north, and vice versa, they often fly on chartered passenger jets the day before and then hole up in one of the best hotels the city has to offer. A couple of seasons ago, Arsenal even flew to nearby Norwich – a journey that takes all of 14 minutes. It's alright for some. The best that the National League can offer is the coach trip. It's not so bad. Sit back, stick on your headphones and let the driver take the strain. Footballers tend to be creatures of habit and everywhere I've played everyone's got their own regular seat, their card school or their particular bunch of mates. There are those who prefer a bit of quiet contemplation and sit alone – those who are up for banter and mucking about. But it's generally been a laid-back atmosphere on the team coaches I've been a part of. The rule of thumb at most of my former clubs was that any trip that took over three hours by coach became an overnight stay. Having said that, one or two of those clubs have gone in for more and more penny-pinching and recently I've been on a coach for four or even five hours without an overnight.

I've spent one of the worst days of my sporting life stranded on a coach. The northern club I was with were playing Sutton in an evening match – a long trip south and we set off at 10.30am. I'd just broken my knee so was on crutches but was going down to give my support to the other lads. I had this big brace on my leg, and it was really hard to get comfortable in my seat. It was a long, long five-hour trip. We then got hammered 4-0, played really badly and the mood on the coach on the way home was grim. It soon got grimmer when 20 minutes' drive outside of Sutton the coach broke down on a roundabout. It took forever for engineers to get to us, and then an age for them to fix it. We ordered a load of delivery pizzas from their local Domino's and twiddled our thumbs for another five hours. Two of the lads had work the next morning, couldn't wait and legged it off the bus and paid 100 quid each to get the train north. I eventually walked through my door at five the following morning with a very sore and swollen knee.

Another time, we played Weymouth away in an evening match, which was a hell of a journey from the north of England. We travelled the day before, after training on the Monday, and got settled into our hotel. The following morning we woke up – to snow. Lots and lots of snow. Later that morning the match was called off and we had another seven-hour drive back. The match was rearranged for two weeks hence – and again it was snowing in the south-west. The coach was half an hour away from Weymouth when the call came through. Sorry lads, the match has been called off again.

There are some tasty journeys out there, and particularly in the National leagues. It's 276 miles from Dover to Halifax, 247 from Weymouth to Chesterfield, 262 from Torquay to Stockport and 209 miles from Altrincham to Yeovil. Before Barrow made it back into the Football League, they had some whopping journeys to make – 370 miles to Dover, 346 to Weymouth and 350 to Torquay. Even in the National Leagues North and South, which are meant to be more regionalised, there's still a fair amount of travelling. To stack it all up, in the 2019/20 season, in National South, Weymouth had to travel 2,898 miles, while in the National North, Blyth Spartans travelled a whopping 3,582. Blyth's visit to Gloucester City was a near five-hour journey of over 270 miles.

At Tier 6, a lot of the teams are largely made up of part-time players, who all of course have other jobs. Meeting up at 2pm for an away midweek match can be a tough ask if you have employers unsympathetic to the demands of your footballing life. The further you travel away, the earlier in the day you have to set off, which makes things really difficult for some players. I've had team-mates turn up already totally stressed out, after a row with their boss for taking yet more time off. A couple have lost their jobs or quit because of workplace fall-outs over 'that bloody football club'.

When clubs are on tight budgets, coach hire money soon mounts up, particularly if your club is in the extreme north or south. At the end of the season a lot of clubs are looking nervously at who's coming up to see whether they have another long journey on the cards. A few seasons ago Hereford were promoted into the Northern League Premier, which meant a fresh five-and-a-half-hour 280-mile journey for Blyth Spartans. There are a few further-flung football outposts that must spend a fortune on travel. Lowestoft is closer to the Netherlands than to Gloucester and Workington, and Truro and St Ives are a long way from anywhere.

Beneath the National leagues, they tend to be arranged on a much more local basis. But, in reality, further-flung clubs are still looking at trips of one or two hours each way. For a lot of smaller clubs, travel costs sit above player payments and gas and electricity bills as their biggest expenditure. Further down the pyramid, some clubs have turned down promotion after doing their sums, realising they'd be paying significantly more on travel if they went up. Its sheer economics but a real shame for the players who've been battling all season to get into the promotion places and the fans who were looking forward to seeing them in a higher league. I really feel for the boards who have to make those decisions. They have the future of the club at heart but end up pleasing no one.

Unless clubs are playing far away in a cup match, the only ones who are afforded the 'luxury' of overnight stays are broadly in the National League. At all the clubs I've played for, we've always stayed in pretty decent hotels. I'd say National League clubs in the main treat their players and staff well when they're on the road. I think I'm right in saying that the ruling body has a list of most-favoured hotels that they give to clubs, and most teams tend to stick to these. But sometimes not ...

We played Torquay away, couldn't get into the hotel we usually used and ended up in a random B&B. The place was falling apart. I had a broken toilet, no hot water and the lights wouldn't work in any of our rooms. And they'd no idea how to cater for a football team. The night before the match, the only options they had were fish and chips or burgers, and trifle for dessert. We all suspected that the owners were Torquay fans.

Further north, we stayed at a hotel just off the A1 the night before a match with Gateshead. It was truly disgusting. The rooms clearly hadn't been cleaned for days. There were smears of blood on my bathroom sink, and the shower was filthy and clogged up with locks of hair. The sheets on my bed were ripped and suspiciously stained, and the pillowcases smelled of really cheap and nasty perfume. You don't even want to think about it. We all complained like hell and let every single National League club know about the dump, so they'd never stay there in the future. That's a lot of parties of 20-plus, so more fool them for being such a crap hotel.

You always share with a room-mate and at every club I've played for I've gone out of my way to find a like-minded soul who was into the quiet life. I never wanted to be up until three in the morning playing cards, or FIFA on the Xbox like some of the players did, who'd then come down for breakfast next morning looking like death warmed up. I saw staying away for the night as purely functional. Eat a meal, watch some telly, get a good night's sleep. Play football, go home.

It must be said, though, that non-league football does wonders for your knowledge of English geography. When you play league football you tend to visit big cities and large towns, that you know of or have heard of before. My experience of non-league was often of travelling to places I hadn't a clue about. Marine – where the hell's that? It's in Crosby on Merseyside, north of Bootle and south of Southport. Brackley anyone? A small market town in Northamptonshire. The first time we saw Forest Green Rovers on the fixture list was a total head-scratcher. Everyone drew a blank trying to find the town of Forest Green on Routefinder. It was only when we googled Forest Green Rovers themselves that we discovered the club was based in the tiny Gloucestershire town of Nailsworth. The joke is I've travelled to all of these places and hundreds more and seen nothing of the towns and cities I've visited. You get off the coach, walk a few metres into a football stadium and then do it in reverse at the end of the match. Sightseeing is most definitely not on the agenda, particularly in Luton.

Playing down in Tier 8 as I do now, most of our away matches are within an hour of the ground, so there's a lot less travel. I don't miss it one little bit. Over 15 years of playing the game you grow weary of the same hotels, the same routines and the snoring team-mates. Staying in a hotel is great when you're on holiday and you're there to relax. But for me, as a footballer, an overnight stay is strictly work-related and I'm 'on duty' the second we arrive.

Fans

I LOVE fans. They're the lifeblood of the game. Why would we play football if it wasn't to entertain an audience? From when I was young, having family, friends and other spectators on the touchline drove me to want to play football for a living. To play well and please other people became a drug for me. It's how I imagine it is like being an actor. People watch you and if you perform well they get a lot of joy from it. They feel proud about it and you can feel proud about yourself. Without fans, what's the point of football? Playing in front of empty terraces during the pandemic certainly drove that home.

In the main, non-league fans rightly have a reputation for being uber-loyal and committed to their clubs, which tend to be much more rooted in their local communities than the top clubs. You sense a much greater camaraderie and togetherness amongst the fans because it's 'their club'. It's personal, in the blood. It's embarrassing to admit, but as a player you too often take for granted the massive difference the fans make at the non-league level because they don't simply come to watch the matches, many of them give up large amounts of their time to volunteer.

The smaller the club the more vital the volunteers become, because when an outfit has little or no full-time or paid staff it's the fans that pick up the slack. I've been at clubs where volunteers have done the accounts, ordered stock for the bar, washed the team kit, painted the stands and the dressing rooms, sold the pies, run the turnstiles and maintained the pitch. They've acted as stewards, served behind the bar, sold the programmes and souvenirs. Not only are they not paid a penny, but often end up out of pocket. At some clubs, fans put in more hours than they would in a full-time paid job. It's that kind of dedication that makes non-league fans something special.

Whenever I signed for a new club I always thought about the fans. I might only be with them for a season or two, but they've been backing their club for years. Often, generations of the same family have formed the bedrock of support for teams and it's at the heart of their identity and what they're about. Grandads and grandmas have passed on the love for their club to the next generation and the one after that. People who reckon football is just a game really don't get it. There's a heritage here, particularly in non-league, that binds families, friends and communities together in a really important way. Football has always been about much more than the match on the pitch.

Players shouldn't take that lightly. As a professional, you have to give of your best, wherever you shore up. It's important to remember just what your new club means to its supporters. Just by the law of averages, most clubs have had little success. We all want to win but most of the time we don't. Every season only one club wins their league or their cup. For non-league fans that means many fallow years of mediocrity and struggle. And yet they still turn up and support their team, putting time, energy and money into helping out. I think it's really important that players understand that and take nothing for granted when they walk out on to the pitch of their new clubs. We're here, because they're there.

Most of the time, I've had a great relationship with fans at all of my clubs – in one case, I ended up lodging with some. That was down in the Midlands. A lovely middle-aged couple who were lifelong fans of my team and totally committed to grassroots football. I ended up watching and helping out with the Sunday league teams they ran. I'd often hand out trophies at their prize-giving nights and I loved being a link to the club. It was a joy to feel their enthusiasm and dedication towards the team I was now playing for. I enjoyed so many after-match chats with them. Talking through the match, my feelings and theirs about it, a rare experience of getting thinking fans' genuine points of view on what they saw from the stands. They made me think a lot about the matches I was playing in. I still keep in contact with them and several other individual fans from two or three of the clubs I've spent time at. These are the real fans of the game.

But taking off those rose-tinted spectacles for a moment, I can't say that all is sweetness and light. Some fans aren't quite so friendly. In the old Conference and now in the National leagues, the nastiest tended to be at ex-Football League clubs such as York, Grimsby, Wrexham, Stockport and Luton. Playing away at those clubs has always been fun and games. I think it's a pride thing. Supporters have seen them being competitive in Leagues One and Two, even the Championship, and now they're watching their clubs playing at their lowest-ever levels. Although scrapping and fights are fairly rare at non-league matches, they're not unknown. Over the years, I've witnessed some fairly tasty dust-ups in the stands – and been in the middle of a couple off the pitch.

I've fallen foul of Luton fans twice. The first was during a match that was petering out into a draw. In the dying stages, one of their midfielders whipped in a low cross from the right. I launched myself at the ball to clear but made a real pig's ear of it and diverted the cross into the path of a Luton player. He swung a boot and in it went. My momentum took me smack bang into a crumpled heap against the advertising hoardings at the Luton end.

Now, bearing in mind I'm the opposition player whose mistake has just handed their team the win, the Luton hardcore spilled out on to the edge of the pitch and totally set about me. While I lay prone on the ground, I was repeatedly punched, kicked, pushed and pulled around like a rag doll and given dog's own abuse. A mix of stewards and my own players managed to pull me out of there, thank god. I suffered regular nightmares about that incident. Red, angry, pissed-up faces contorted with fury and hatred stuck right in my face, showering me with gob and vitriol. And I'd effectively won the match for them.

We returned to Luton the following season and, in front of a big noisy crowd, managed to come out on top in a fractious, hard-fought battle of a match. The Luton fans weren't happy bunnies. Some of our players had driven down, so they legged it quick sharp out of the stadium and gunned their cars out of Kenilworth Road as fast as they could. The rest of us trooped out to our waiting coach under a hail of abuse, and while we waited for the last of our club's staff to board, a mob of angry Luton fans surrounded our bus. Most of our players stuck on their headphones to drown out the noise, but soon we could feel the coach being punched and rocked. As I pulled off my phones, a brick came flying through a window just in front of me. I was showered with glass, as were several of my team-mates. Coach windows are toughened and double-glazed, so to smash one requires throwing a brick with some degree of force and anger.

The poor driver was crapping himself. He hadn't signed up for this – and neither had we. Obviously, he couldn't drive us back up north with a smashed window, so he had to call for a replacement coach. Around us, all hell was kicking off with the Luton fans, so the police arrived to protect us. I can't tell you how relieved we were to see the replacement bus arrive. But it didn't end there. The police were still so concerned about our safety that they gave us an escort out of the town and on to the motorway. I was bloody glad to get home that night.

It's not just away fans that can give you major grief. At one of my clubs, a former Football League club, the fans were brutal with their own. It's such hard work playing in front of an unforgiving crowd. If you were 1-0 down at half-time, they'd be booing you off. They didn't like being in the Conference one little bit, and they weren't used to losing against non-league teams. It would be ringing in your ears when you ran off at half-time. 'X, you're fucking shit.' 'X, you're a fucking disgrace to the shirt.' And the worst: 'X, I hope you fucking die of cancer.' And this to their own player. You know, I get it. Fans might have had a crap week at work and going to the match is a great way to let off steam. They pay their hard-earned money to watch you, and when it's not going well, it's no surprise when they get annoyed. Emotions can run high in football.

But if only they realised how much it can affect you inside, they'd maybe dial down the hate speech. As a player, you accept that if the team is playing badly, the fans have every right to give you the boos. But when it becomes personal, they're hurting their team. You can have the hide of a rhino, but when you're getting such personal stick, it does knock you back. It genuinely puts a negative nervous energy into your body. I'm quite mentally tough, but I'll be honest, the fans at this club really got to me. You'd see an ambitious long pass or the opportunity for a clever one-two. Then you'd think twice. What if it doesn't come off? Will the boo-boys be on my back again? It certainly made me play in my shell more often than I'd wish to admit, and so I'd go for the shorter ball or the safer option. I wanted to do well for the fans and succeed at that club, but their constant abuse made me desperate not to fail. Ergo, play safe.

I've often gone home from matches like this feeling really down. When your own fans slag you, it's a horrible feeling and stays with you for days afterwards. You're doing your best for them and, okay, you might make mistakes, maybe not perform at your peak, but you're still striving, still desperate to do your best. What really hurts is when fans go online to say it looked as if you weren't really trying. Football is an utterly unpredictable game and, hey, guess what, sometimes the opposition have done a far better job of managing the match than your team. As an individual player, that can take you out of the action, because they've targeted you. In the creative midfield position I've always played in, I've often had two players on me, but I still had slags saying I couldn't get a grip on the match. When you have two players continually on your back, that's tough to do.

I can't think of any other job where you turn up with the intention of entertaining people and get dog's abuse. They say football is the theatre of the people. Can you imagine going to the theatre, standing up in the middle of a play and screaming at the top of your lungs that the leading man is a useless twat?

When I first started out as a pro, social media and club chat forums were just becoming popular. I used to see them as a great way for players to communicate with fans and vice versa. They'd ask me what I thought of a particular match we might have played, and I'd give them my honest views. Yes, I think we should have had a penalty in the second half. No, we pushed up too much in the first. And, often, the poster would thank you for being so frank.

As things progressed, the 'thank yous' became non-existent. Instead, I was a twat, fuck off out of our club. Increasingly, the forums became evil stuff, really personal. Like all players, I've had my fair share of threatening posts. 'If I ever see you out in town, I'm gonna punch your fucking lights out.' 'Never come in such and such a pub, cos we'll have you.' There was even a death threat or two. Bearing in mind, this isn't Barcelona or Roma, it's non-league football.

What would really get to me – and still does – is how some fans go after young players just starting their careers. A kid could be making his first steps into proper adult football. Like us all when we're finding our way, he's going to make mistakes, make wrong decisions and sometimes get so bloody nervous that he doesn't look for the ball. When they get slated and abused by their own fans it can totally crush their confidence. Social media and the amount of time most young players spend on it seems to have made this ten times worse.

The joke is that 99 per cent of these people have never played, coached or managed football at a serious level and clearly don't understand how the game is played. But social media has allowed them to become instant experts. It's often laughable to read their views on tactics, players' abilities and how matches should be played. They generally have no idea. But that's not the worst that comes back at footballers from keyboard warriors.

I've played alongside and against a lot of black footballers. As we sadly know, the online racial abuse that players get is huge. I've really felt for team-mates of mine who've been targeted with such prejudiced filth. For me, taking the knee is the least any reasonable and decent footballer can do to show their solidarity. I was very happy to see the West Brom fan who racially abused Romaine Sawyers online get an eight-week prison sentence, and I sincerely hope it serves as a wake-up call to other racist fans.

I'm older and wiser and rarely respond to the garbage online these days. The worst, of course, always comes on a Saturday or midweek night after a match. And as the night goes on and the fans get ever more drunk, the worse the posts. It's often ignorant and wrong. There was one guy a couple of years ago who was totally – and very abusively – on my case again and again for not setting up enough goals from midfield. But I ended that season with 18 assists! I really feel for some of the top players who seem to be the focus of constant social media abuse. It doesn't matter how much you're paid, when those levels of vitriol and hatred are being directed your way, it must have major knock-on effects with your mental health.

I think there's much more cynicism at the top levels of the game on so many fronts, which could well be why I've noticed an increasing trend – the number of fans who've become fed up with forking out up to two grand a year for Premier League season tickets and found a new home in non-league football. Fans who feel their club doesn't give a damn about the reasons for their passion and support and only wants their money. They've discovered a world where crowd segregation is almost unheard of and at a lot of grounds you can stand on the terraces wherever you want, with a beer in your hand. They're finding out too that most non-league football clubs don't treat you like a wallet to be emptied at every opportunity. Food and drink are a lot more economically priced and match tickets are comparatively cheap. Because many of the grounds are small, you're close to the action, which adds to the immediacy of the experience. Okay, so the quality of the game at non-league level may not be as great but, in most cases, it's not kick and rush and there's a lot of skill and talent on show.

Over the last four or five years – Covid aside – attendances have been on a healthy upward trend across non-league football clubs in general. In the National League alone, crowds have gone up by an average 10 per cent. If clubs are going to survive the economic effects of the pandemic, long may that continue. I truly believe that more and more football fans will turn to non-league, because they want to feel like they 'belong' to a club.

'Ultra' groups are springing up all over non-league, most opposed to the over-commercialisation of football. Dulwich Hamlet's Champion Hill ground in National League South is home to 'The Rabble', who have their own podcast, website and fanzine. Even down in the ninth tier, Eastbourne Town has The Pier Pressure Ultras, who make matchdays something different with their saxophones and drums. The ultras have helped bring more atmosphere into the grounds generally. As a player, there's nothing quite like seeing the flares and smoke under the floodlights and hearing the chanting when you run out for a night match. But I'll be truthful, once you've kicked off the crowd immediately fades far away into the background. Most of the time, you're concentrating so hard on the flow of the match and thinking about what you need to do next that you're not aware of the fans. It's not that you're consciously trying to blank them out, it's that your total focus is on the match. The moments when crowd noise really cuts through is when you've scored a goal or won a penalty or a free kick, and that's when the fans really lift you. That's real butterflies time. Or, more negatively, when you hear your name because the fans are on your back. But I'd rather hear the catcalls than play in an empty stadium.

My experience of playing without fans wasn't a happy one. Okay, so if you make a blunder there's only the other players and the coaching staff who'll see it. But a match without a crowd is a depressing affair. I had to work a lot harder at lifting myself for matches, because the atmosphere was so non-existent. It felt as if you were playing a behind-doors friendly or a training match. Whichever way you slice it, football is all about the fans.

There's no denying that football fans can be bloody witty. Fan banter in non-league grounds has had me cut up many times in the past. A chant that York City fans sang at smaller away grounds was: 'My garden shed is bigger than this.' I remember when North Ferriby had their one season in the sun in the National League, fans at my ex-club sang, 'What's it like to see a crowd?' That did cut through to me on the pitch. As it did when Forest Green Rovers visited and their fans were regaled with chants of, 'If it wasn't for the hippy, you'd be shit.' And hats off to the Blyth fan who screamed out his assessment of the referee's attempts at sorting out a defensive wall in a match against Marine a few years ago: 'If that's ten yards then I'm not letting you measure my carpets.' Incidentally, at Blyth's local rivals Gateshead the fans sing, and I have no idea why, the old Laurel and Hardy classic 'The Blue Ridge Mountains of Virginia'. I think that sense of wit and bonhomie has also been attracting more fans to non-league.

A lot of big-club fans are also adopting non-league clubs as their 'second' teams, thanks in part to Non-League Day, which has been running successfully since 2010. Timed to coincide with a weekend where the Premier League and Championship are on an international break, fans without a match to attend are encouraged to try out their nearest local non-league side. Clubs up and down the pyramid look to Non-League Day for a boost in attendances and many offer reduced admission prices and special deals. Some clubs have offered very offbeat deals on Non-League Day. Down towards the bottom end of the pyramid in the Anglian Combination Division Two, Bungay Town FC doubled the usual size of their crowd to 100 by offering free punnets of mushrooms to fans.

Non-League Day is also the prime opportunity to reach out to a potential new audience, vital to the future of our leagues – kids. In 2021, Dagenham & Redbridge ran a 'Kids 4 a Quid' offer, while Lancaster City in the NPL let under-14s in for free. A number of other clubs ran similar schemes because they see what I see – crowds of mainly older faces.

This is a big worry of mine for non-league football. Twenty years ago, you didn't have to walk far to see a bunch of kids kicking a football around. It's much rarer now. There are so many other leisure pursuits and distractions for children these days, most of which they don't even need to leave their homes to get involved in. From Gameboy and Netflix, to e-sports and social media, kids can sit in their rooms to connect with the outside world. Much less fun to go out into the cold and rain to play with your mates when you can play with them online in the warmth and comfort of your own home.

They're losing their connection with football. When they do have any, it's with the glamour and 'showbiz' of the Premier League – the replica shirts and big-screen live matches. In comparison, non-league must look old and outdated, like another world. The game has to work ever harder at growing that next generation of fans. That's why it's so important that non-league clubs dig down ever deeper into their local communities. We have to find a way of connecting with children and making them realise that not all football is about who's the richest, the most successful, the most glamorous. Non-league is about a sense of belonging.

In this respect, another worry of mine is the increasing amount of 'player churn'. Most National League footballers are now on one-year contracts, some as short as six months, and that's if they have a contract at all. Players move into a club and then move on with alarming regularity. It's no longer rare these days to see footballers who've played for 15–20 non-league teams by the end of their careers. It makes life easier for clubs that might need to tighten their belts. No one has to be paid off and if the board need to reduce the player budget they can get rid of higher earners sooner rather than later. Needless to say, this makes life very unstable and precarious for the players. But for fans, it becomes increasingly harder to identify with the men out on the pitch. In pre-season, some clubs are replacing as many as 15 or 16 players in their squads. So, it's hard to have favourites and heroes out there on the pitch, when it'll be Mr A.N. Other a few months later.

When it feels as if the players are perpetual nomads who continually move from club to club, it must be hard to feel connected to your team. Unfortunately, these days it's only fans who can afford to be loyal to their clubs. Players must make a living and if clubs, for whatever reason, aren't prepared to extend short contracts, then players have no alternative but to move on. This has happened to me a couple of times and, as a player, you get little or no chance to truly connect with the fans. I'm now on my tenth club and the contracts were all a lot lengthier earlier in my career. As a child, I used to watch footballers who were 'one-club players'. I doubt those days will ever return to the world of non-league football.

Managers

OVER THE years, non-league football has produced some impressive managers and management teams. Premier League and Championship bosses such as Ron Atkinson (Kettering Town), Neil Warnock (Gainsborough Trinity) and Steve Evans (Stamford) all cut their teeth in the old Conference leagues. More recently, the Cowley brothers made a great name for themselves at Concord, Braintree and Lincoln.

There are also living legends such as Jim Gannon and Rudy Funk. A grizzled centre-half, Gannon turned out for Stockport County 383 times in the old First and Second divisions and over the years since has gone on to manage them three times, and much of that time in non-league. Gannon isn't a shrinking violet and has had a string of public fallings-out with players, chairmen, opposition managers, referees and authority in general. One of his former players at Stockport told me Gannon refused to be interviewed by Sky Sports because Sky hadn't fixed his Sky box. One of the few managers in non-league to hold a full UEFA Pro Licence, he's now the boss at Northern Premier League Hyde United.

If you're not aware of Rudy Funk, welcome to the slightly eccentric side of non-league football. A huge fan favourite, he's managed all over non-league for the likes of Long Eaton, Shirebrook, Rainworth Miners Welfare, Eastwood Town, Scarborough and Mansfield. A former handball coach from Romania and an inveterate smoker, Funk is a manager who's often rung his players the night before a match to say he loves them, imploring each individual to win the match for the man who loves you all.

Like anywhere in football, the non-league pyramid has, and still does, contain the good, the bad, the ugly – and the just plain bloody awful. I've played under all four. Let's start with a heart-warming positive. As I've already alluded to, the best manager I've ever worked with is Gary Mills, and that's bearing in mind that early in my career I was managed for a short while by a former England manager. Gary Mills played well over 200 league matches at right-back and in midfield at Nottingham Forest and Leicester in the old First Division and then the Premier League. Aged 18, he was the youngest player to appear in a European Cup final, when Forest beat Hamburger SV 1-0 in 1980. After his playing career finished, he managed York and Notts County in League Two; in non-league, his management jobs included stints at Alfreton, Wrexham, York, Tamworth and Gateshead. I, for one, continue to be amazed that Gary hasn't bossed at a much higher level.

I joined the club he was managing at the time after suffering a really tough season under a manager that not only didn't understand me and what I offered as a player but wouldn't talk to me either. We'll dissect all that a little later in this chapter, because it's an object lesson in how not to manage footballers. I arrived low in confidence but desperate to get myself back on track. I couldn't have been luckier. Gary Mills instilled a new belief in me, believed in my ability and made me feel like a million dollars as a player. When a manager shows faith and appreciation in your skills, you in turn want to give back to that manager, and that's exactly what happened with Gary Mills. He actually converted me into a holding midfielder, a position I'd never played before, but it worked to perfection and I excelled in my spell under him.

Training was a joy. Mills made it interesting, exciting. All the lads enjoyed training as it was so different to your usual structured and boring drills. Some days he'd give us a ball each and then set us a series of challenges. First off, hit the crossbar from outside the area. Once you'd managed that you moved on to the next challenge, which might be a half-volley into the net without a bounce, and so on. On the surface, it might just have appeared a 'fun' circuit. There was certainly plenty of banter between the players. But it was highly competitive, and the lads loved it. Underneath the laughs, he was getting us to improve our technical skills and encourage quick one- and two-touch football.

That might be the Monday after a Saturday match and then he'd say, 'See you Thursday lads,' and give us two days off. Then you'd come in on the Thursday, totally buzzing and up for it. The training would be really high-tempo, and everyone was raring to go for Saturday again. Gary Mills made you want to give everything for him, because of the way he treated you. His game plans for individual matches were always clear and well thought-out. It seemed to me that every player jogged out on to the pitch understanding exactly what was being asked of them. That was certainly the case with me.

Sadly, Mills moved on and so did I. Another couple of short one-year contracts and then I found myself struggling to get a new club. Bills needed paying and the money was running out. A smaller club in the National League came in for me. Amazingly, they were offering more money than I'd been paid at my previous, bigger club. Initially, it all sounded very encouraging. The owner was a successful local businessman who financially backed the outfit to the extent that all the playing staff were totally full-time. The gaffer had previously managed in the Football League, and although this wasn't particularly successfully, my hopes were that his track record meant he was experienced enough at a higher level to have picked up some fresh ideas and ambition. The season before, I'd played my new club twice and they were awful, dreary long-ball stuff. But now the manager had decided to play football on the ground and get players in with good ball skills and ability. Music to my ears.

The guy's training sessions were very old school and dull, and he didn't seem to have much insight into tactics and match planning. But hey, he was allowing me to play my own game. I started the first six matches and did pretty well. A couple of man-of-the-matches, some good assists. Unfortunately, despite my best efforts, our football wasn't translating into results and the manager decided to rip up his 'playing it around on the floor' plan. That was me done. From then on, it was lump it upfield. I soon became, in the manager's words 'a luxury player' and soon found myself on the bench. Sometimes he left me out completely.

As things do on the football grapevine, word came back to me from a couple of players who'd been with my manager at his Football League club. According to both, he was the worst they'd ever played under but, at the time, their club was on a downward spiral, totally skint, and although he was cheap, they couldn't afford to buy him out of his contract. My heart sank further. Under his new route-one policy, results didn't improve. So, one week he announced an 11 vs 11 match in training, and he announced that the best

11 from that match would get picked on Saturday. A clean slate for everyone. Afterwards, all the lads were patting me on the back, saying I'd been the best player on the pitch. Come Saturday, I wasn't even on the bench. I was sitting in the stands.

His team talks used to demoralise me. 'Every time you get the ball, kick it as far as you can.' 'Never hang on to the ball. One touch, then kick it long.' The more time I spent on the bench or in the stands, the more I saw him at work first-hand. He was a Neanderthal. One of our players broke an opponent's nose during a match. The manager gave him a wink, a grin and a thumbs-up and then shouted, 'Well done, son.' If anyone managed to injure an opponent off the ball, he'd be gleeful. 'Break his fucking leg next time.' And honestly, he meant it. A former professional player himself, who knew how that could wreck a career and destroy a livelihood. But he meant it.

His idea of man management merely extended to berating his own players. During one match, he decided to go after our centre-forward, constantly screaming, 'You're a fucking thick cunt!' He was on his case for the entire match. Never shouting match instructions or advice about how to change his game – just 'you're a fucking thick cunt' again and again. It's bad enough when your own fans are knocking your confidence by giving you totally mindless, unhelpful stick, but when it's your own manager? True motivational genius. I remember thinking, *I wonder what the fans make of this?* They could clearly hear him; it wasn't Old Trafford. What if his family are sat behind the dugout? His kids? What about the loads of kids that were there? Shouting that at one of his own players, incredible. These aren't the kind of people I'll miss when I've finished my career.

He started signing new players. The first was a goalie and the manager's first priority was to get hold of one who could hoof the ball hard and long. Not was he a good shot stopper, decent positionally or handy at commanding his box, but could he boot the ball 70 yards? I knew my number was up when he signed two new 'midfielders' – both of them 6ft 4in centre-halves who'd never played in the middle of the pitch. Their simple mission? 'Search and destroy'. And 'just fucking hoof it'. In terms of technical ability, one of them was the worst footballer I've ever played with. A lovely lad, but fair to say you wouldn't want him on your five-a-side team. He was an athlete who'd kick it quick and long, but couldn't trap a bag of cement, never mind pass a ball.

For our next away match, I was left out again, but was told I had to travel, even though I'd just be sitting in the stands. Even in those circumstances, I'd still keep myself ticking over, by having a good hard run on the pitch before and after a match. But this particular time, knowing I wasn't picked, I'd spent a couple of gruelling days in the gym, really going for it. I decided to have the 'weekend off' and knock the running on the head at the match.

Come the match, I was sitting up in the stands again. We were beaten 3-0 and were truly dreadful. Monday morning in training the manager got us all together and went ballistic. He had a real go at the team that had been out on the pitch – and then laid into me! Slagged me off for not showing commitment, sitting on my lazy backside in the stands and not bothering to go for my post-match runs. I told him about going mad at the gym, but he wasn't listening, just off on one. And then I lost it. I had a pop back at him in front of the rest of the lads, something I'd never done. I fixed him with a death stare and said, 'You can say you don't like me as a player, but you'll never EVER question my attitude or professionalism again!'

As soon as I'd said it, I don't know who was more shocked, him or the lads. But I'm guessing it was him, because he had nothing to come back with at all. None of the lads could believe he'd actually tried to blame a shambolic 3-0 hammering on the players he'd left in the stand for the match. The January transfer window was coming up. I told my agent in no uncertain terms to get me out of there. Two days later I was on my way, hoping that I'd never meet that jerk again.

Sometimes you get a call that blows your socks off. Earlier in my career I'd been offered a contract extension at the northern club I played for and was mulling it over when my agent rang with a very bright timbre to his voice. This was unusual. His phone manner was usually very businesslike and quite downbeat. The news was that another Conference club were in for me. A former league club, they now found themselves floating around the bottom of the Conference and had decided to sack their manager mid-season. They were offering more money, a better all-round deal, and their new manager, a former Championship player, was a big fan of mine. I was, my agent told me, the first on the list of players he wanted to sign. So, what do you do? Well, of course, you go for the meeting.

My agent and I sat there waiting in the manager's office. He was running late. It was all busy, busy. Finally, he arrived, totally coordinated in sight and smell – expensive suit and aftershave. He enthusiastically shook my hand and perched on the edge of his desk. 'This time I'm having you,' he said. 'I've tried to sign you three times before. But now, I'm having you.'

He was flash as fuck and clearly loved himself. But this guy had a hell of a track record as a player and I was feeling very flattered. The manager laid out his plans. I was one of the best players he'd seen in the Conference. If I signed, I'd be the first name on the team sheet every week. My agent kept throwing me approving looks and the man in the Armani suit continued to ask me for pen on paper. I said I'd think about it. Needed to talk further with my agent. 'Okay,' the manager said with a grin, 'but I know you'll sign. I need you, man!'

I talked to my dad on the phone later and he was as cautious as ever. 'Don't jump at it,' he said. My agent put it to me straight – just sign. This is a really good deal with an ex-Football League club who are desperate to get back there. They've got the money, the clout and the manager. Next year, you could be back in League Two. He was right. What could possibly go wrong?

I signed, a happy chappie. This new club wasn't that far away from where I lived at the time, so I didn't have to move home yet again. Just a short 40-minute commute to training every day. I arrived at the first training session with a happy heart. Until our manager sat us down.

We had two weeks without a match when I first arrived, and he said the squad weren't fit enough – the usual clichéd crap that new managers say when they inherit a team that's not doing so well. So, on the Monday morning we were sent out on a five-mile run to a local gym. As soon as everyone had made it, we were thrust straight into a one-hour body-pump session, which if you've experienced one, you'll know what a killer it is. With little break, we then had to run the five miles back to the ground, but this time we were on the clock. Unless every single member of the squad made it back by a given time, we'd have to spend another half an hour running around the ground. We literally had to push the lads who were poor runners or just plain lazy, and just scraped it. We were banned from eating carbs after 6pm, so we came back the following morning and everyone was dying. Hamstrings screaming, tight calves and fatigue from the lack of carbs. The manager decided in his (lack of) wisdom that we should all do bleep tests – and this is on already sore and knackered legs. We then had a second football and running session in the afternoon. The whole two weeks before our next match was double fitness and training sessions every day and we got ruined. My body fat dropped to 5 per cent, the lowest I'd ever been. My partner said I just looked ill. Did it work? Did it bollocks. We still had a stinker with him in charge.

There were a lot of tweaks and injuries. He was reckless, unsystematic. Arrogantly thought he'd picked up chapter and verse about every new training method going, but either cherry-picked or totally misunderstood what they were really about. No one was allowed to criticise. He was the great 'I am'. 'I've played football at a level none of you'll ever reach.' He'd boast about how much he'd earned from his career and act flash. But then turn up every day in a used runabout! He'd tell us he'd played under top managers and coaches who taught him a hundred times more than anything we'd ever know. This is when I began to think, if that's the case, why are you managing at your third non-league club?

The dressing room was a war zone. The manager had made it very clear that he had his coterie of favourites, and the rest had better fall in with that or else. I soon realised that, despite everything he'd told me, I was neither his first name on the team sheet nor one of his favourites. He loved conflict amongst the players and believed it kept us all sharp.

It didn't. Unhappy? Angry? Frustrated? Demotivated? Yes, all of those would do.

We played Luton at home. A big match and, for the Conference, a big crowd. First half, I played really well. We went in 0-0. To my shock and utter surprise, the manager immediately got into my face, screaming and shouting at me. I was recoiling back as his spit was spraying all over my eyes and my mouth. I was rubbish, selfish, shite. He was effing and jeffing at me and I had no idea why. A nearby team-mate shook his head and muttered I was our best player. And so, he got a mouthful of spit. The manager took me off early in the second half and didn't even acknowledge me as I trotted off. Just turned away from me. I was at a complete loss. After the match, a couple of the Luton staff said they couldn't believe he'd replaced me. They were chuffed to bits, because up until then I'd easily been the best player on the pitch. Whatever, I knew that as a player I'd lost the manager and he'd lost me. And it frustrated the life out of me because all I was trying to do was be committed and professional. I've never been a player who tries to play mind games. Unlike the manager.

He was a gambler who constantly needed money. If the manager was short, he'd dip into the players' fines pot, which was meant to pay for our Christmas do. On Wednesdays, lads who hadn't played in the previous match had to come in for an extra day of training to keep them fit. He soon let it be known that if they slipped him 50 quid each, they could have that day off. Looking from the outside, I thought it stank – a manager sponging off his players and offering favours for cash.

At another club, we had a player who came from a well-known local criminal family. He could get you anything at knock-off prices, but most of us wouldn't touch it. We knew it was nicked gear. So did our manager, but that didn't over-worry his moral compass. He used the lad to get him Christmas presents on the cheap – games, computer consoles, that kind of thing. This bloke hadn't had a sniff at the first team before then. Funnily enough, he soon started to get regular run-outs.

As the season went on at that club, life became a joke. The manager's assistant delivered the worst training sessions of my entire career. If you can imagine the most unstructured sessions in your life, that was him. There never seemed to be any point to the challenges and routines he'd give us. He'd try to explain them, and we'd be none the wiser. He once told us he borrowed a lot of his training session ideas from Real Madrid, and we just pissed ourselves laughing. He had no idea how to organise players and, as he was in his seventies and waiting for a hip replacement, he couldn't demo anything to us. I'm not making light of his health problems, but he shouldn't have been on the training pitch with us, he should have been off sick. He hadn't a clue how much or how little training we needed at any given time, so generally you never even broke into a sweat. As a player, it's utterly depressing when you have a coach that you know can't train you properly.

Come February/March time, we were well and truly mired in a relegation battle, and I'd become a regular on the bench. *Never mind*, I thought, *at least I've still got a year left on my contract.* So, there I am, driving home one day, and the assistant rang me, which was unheard of: 'You won't play much for us again,' he told me, 'so I've been having words with a few people I know. Belper Town are keen to take you on and they'll pay £150 a week.'

For a while, I was speechless. 'Are you serious? That's two levels lower than us and they're offering a fifth of what

I'm currently earning. Why for one second would you think I'd be remotely interested in such a crap deal? Christ, what would you do if you were offered that?' And I clicked off my phone, bloody fuming. A few days later, he tried it on again. I can't remember what club it was, but again they were much lower than us in the non-league pyramid and were offering peanuts. I said, 'Are you taking the mickey out of me? Shit money at a club that are bloody miles away. I'll never ever do that. Just what is wrong with you?'

Not surprisingly, we ended that season in big trouble. Injuries and suspensions meant I was temporarily back in the team and I was determined to show everyone I deserved to be wearing that shirt again. For the first 45 minutes, I played pretty well. At half-time, the manager came up to me, the centre-half and the centre-forward and out of nowhere called us all 'snakes'. We didn't know at the time, but if we lost that match he was going to get the sack and I think he thought we knew. We had one player in the dressing room who was a little snitch and would report back anything he heard to the manager's assistant. No doubt we'd been heard slagging him off a few times, because he was a terrible manager with a dreadful assistant and he probably thought we were revelling in his misfortune. I went out for the second half and the ref, who I knew from a good few past matches, had heard everything through the wall. He was aghast. 'Did I hear that right? Did he really call you a snake? You! You're probably the nicest lad I've met in football. How could he call you that?'

After the match, the assistant manager had a real go at our centre-forward for not holding the ball up enough, and the lad just snapped: 'Why don't you just fuck off! I'm sick to death of hearing your stupid voice, week in, week bloody out!' I'd never seen the assistant look so shocked.

He told us not to worry about relegation. 'Because I'm here, and I've never been relegated.' He was that season.

Although these two were nasty, shouty, ignorant bastards, funnily enough they're not the worst kind of manager you can get. The pits is the boss who won't talk. A few years ago, I was at a northern club in the Conference. The season before had been a good one for me. I was in the top three in the player of the season fans' poll and had a string of man-of-the-match performances under my belt. We'd challenged at the top for most of the season but fell off coming towards securing a play-off place. We ended up a few points short in ninth place. Shame about the ending, although not a bad season overall for the club or for me.

The board didn't agree. A former league club, they were desperate to be back in League Two and felt they needed a new manager with enough ambition to get them there. On paper, the new man looked really promising. He'd coached at much higher levels and managed in League Two. I knew his philosophy of trying to play football on the ground, which really suited my style of play from midfield. In truth, I was looking forward to working with him. But things started to get a little ominous for me in pre-season. The very first thing he did was to buy other players in my position, and after having been an ever-present the season before, from match one of the new campaign I became a bench-warmer. I spent my first eight matches as a sub and never got brought on once. Not for a second.

The new guy playing in my position was bang average, so I couldn't get it. Why was the new manager not playing me? For the first time in my career I asked for a personal meeting with the boss. I was a play-it-on-the-ground wide midfielder – was the new manager looking for something different? I didn't know, because he'd never ever spoken to me. I know that some managers want an out-and-out winger who whips the ball in. But I wasn't watching my replacement doing much of that. All I wanted was ten minutes with the manager to find out where I stood in his future plans. Where was I going wrong? What didn't he like about me as a player? He never responded. But he did send me a very clear message. A week later, I was no longer on the subs' bench, I was watching from the stands. And despite not one word of communication from my new manager, this continued for a few more weeks. Then the youth team manager approached me, obviously feeling very embarrassed. The manager had instructed him to get yours truly training with the youth team on my days off. Aghast, I asked why. 'Sorry, lad. You'll have to ask the manager.'

So again, and again, I tried to do that very thing. But the manager continued to ignore me. I couldn't work it out. I hadn't slept with his wife, killed his dog or robbed his house. Not only did he not know me, he'd never spoken to me. In current parlance, he ghosted me. Nevertheless, I did everything that was asked of me and never moaned. I came in every day and trained with the youth team, as I always had the philosophy that whatever happened and whatever any manager tried to throw at me, I'd continue to be as professional as I could be. You create a bad reputation in football if you spit your dummy out or start acting up, and people talk within football. Managers ring around other managers who've had you previously and they give an opinion. I always felt, naively or not, that even if a gaffer didn't rate me or play me, he'd always at least give me a positive review in terms of being a good pro and a hard worker.

I spent the rest of the season totally out of the picture, angry and utterly frustrated. I had another year on my contract at the club and there's no way I've ever been a player who just picks up a wage. I knew I could offer a lot to the club. But with no communication whatever from the manager, I felt as if I was living in some kind of football purgatory. Can you imagine this in your workplace? Your office, company, factory? You've been working for your boss for nearly a year, made it clear on numerous occasions you want to talk with them about your future – and they still won't talk to you?

Come the close season and totally out of the blue, the manager rang me up. It was literally the first time he'd spoken to me since he arrived at the club. He told me he had no plans to play me in the coming season and I should think about finding a new club. To begin with, I was utterly speechless. So many questions were spinning around in my head. Why haven't you given me run-outs to look at me play? Why don't you like me as a player when you've never picked me for a full match? After making me play with the youth team, he hadn't even seen me train. Then my pride and sense of professionalism kicked in. I told him in no uncertain terms I was only halfway through my contract with the club and I intended to fight for my place in the team. He wished me the best with that and put the phone down.

Although he never gave me a single word about why he didn't fancy me, I realised I was one of his highest earners and guessed he wanted me out to free up funds. I wondered, too, whether he thought I was too lightweight, so I got a weights programme down at my local gym to get bigger, more muscular and worked like a dog on my fitness. Come pre-season, I won every single bleep test. On the ones where he'd have us in groups on staggered starts, I kept catching the other groups up. I triumphed in every single five-mile run, and generally showed myself to be the fittest player at the club. Then it came to the pre-season friendlies and I played out of my skin. In my head, I thought I'd now made the manager look a fool for not picking me before.

But the season started and I was on the bench again. I was in the prime of my career so had to accept that if I was going to play every week, I had to find another club. And to this day, I've no idea what that manager didn't like about me as a player. I'm not including this story as just some personal beef. It's here to give you an idea of how complicated player relationships are with some managers in non-league. I've been at clubs where players were so frozen out that they were banned from talking to other first-team players. Others have been sent off to play for Sunday league teams. All you ask for is some communication, and when that never comes you feel lost.

At my level of the game, you never feel secure. You're always on fairly short-term contracts. In truth, players like me aren't being paid much more than most of the fans who are watching from the terraces – and in quite a few cases, a lot less. I'm not driving home in my Bentley to a millionaire's pad in Wilmslow. I'm trying my best to pay a mortgage for a terraced house and keep my car on the road. It's kept me awake at night many times, not just at that particular club. At non-league level, managers should absolutely know this. So, to not even talk to one of your regular players about their game future with the club shows ignorance, thoughtlessness or just bloody couldn't-give-a-shit callousness.

I've had difficult experiences with team-mates suddenly becoming your manager. It's happened twice to me and both times ended in tears. A guy I'd played alongside for three and a half years and got on very well with was the surprise replacement for our recently sacked manager. He became necessarily distant, but then went too far. I'd been awaiting talks on a new contract and he stalled me and pretty much ignored my agent's calls. Time rolled on, the season was drawing to a close and I remained totally up in the air. Finally, he got one of his assistants to talk with me and offer a much-reduced contract. So reduced that I wouldn't have been able to pay my mortgage. I was furious. As a recent player – and team-mate – he knew how important it was to get contracts sorted as soon as possible. And if agreement couldn't be found, then at least you had a decent amount of time left to find another club. But stalling me for months was unforgiveable. This was my livelihood.

The second former team-mate who made it straight from our dressing room into the manager's seat was a lovely lad who very soon became a victim of his inexperience. He changed the entire spine of the team – goalkeeper, centre-half and centre-forward – in one fell swoop and signed three players who were terrible. We began to sink like a stone, and it killed his fledgling management career. A couple of months later he got the push. I did feel genuinely gutted for him, because he was a great guy. Personally, I think it's a mistake appointing a current player into their first manager's job at their current club. It's so hard to transition from player to manager. Overnight they have to stop being 'one of the lads' and become the disciplinarian, the guy who has to make the tough decisions, and a lot of their former team-mates sometimes find it difficult to accept. If you want to go into management, go elsewhere first and serve your apprenticeship.

And so, we return to Gary Mills. A great communicator who looked after his players, and despite most of his career being played at the highest and most rarefied of levels, took time to understand what life was like for the non-league players he now found himself managing. That's a proper manager. If I ever get into management, I hope the very least I can be is a decent communicator and know what it means to struggle to pay your rent or your mortgage.

Referees

WHO'D BE one? They get dog's own abuse inside and outside the ground, and I know that in the Premier League match officials aren't even allowed to be on social media anymore because of the torrent of aggressive filth and vitriol they used to regularly receive. I've seen referees physically attacked by players, managers and fans alike – now and again all at the same time – and harassed and spat at while getting into their cars. I know some that have received death threats and been told their houses would be burned down because of decisions they'd made in a match. All of this is patently, utterly unacceptable. And, of course, everyone involved in football should remember one simple fact – no referee, no match. But ...

I believe that the general standard of refereeing in this country is poor and it's getting worse from the top down. In 2018, and for the first time in years, no British referees were selected for the World Cup matches in Russia. This is no coincidence. They only choose the best of the best. And if our best aren't good enough to officiate at the top level it surely says something about the standard of referees we currently have down through our divisions into non-league. I can't claim to know why exactly this is the case, but, like any footballer, I have my thoughts.

One of my first chastening experiences of referees as a young professional ended up with me being shown the only red card of my entire career. A team-mate was bearing down on goal, when one of the opposition centre-backs came flying in with a sliding tackle that was all man, no ball. It clearly bloody hurt and, incensed, my midfield mate flew at the defender. Fists were flying and I tried to play peacemaker, wedging myself between the players, pushing them apart. The ref came steaming over, brandishing a red card. Never mind, I thought, I did my best to break up the scrap. But then I realised he wasn't waving the card at either of the other two players. It was me he was sending off. I was aghast.

'No, you've got this all wrong,' I told him. 'I was trying to pull them apart. I was the peacemaker.'

The ref pointed towards the dressing rooms: 'Shut it sonny. And watch the dissent, or I'll card you again.'

I remember trotting off towards the touchline, feeling a huge sense of injustice but also thinking how bloody stupid that referee must have been, not to have had a clear and accurate view of what happened. How can he possibly have got it so wrong? I think that incident made me realise early on just how poor some of the refereeing is in the lower leagues. But it's getting worse. As a player, I've been acutely aware that the standards of refereeing in the National leagues has steadily fallen. It's something that has to change.

There's a hoary old cliché that bad refereeing decisions even themselves out over a season. As a player, I can tell you that's complete bollocks. I've been in promotion and relegation battles where I've almost dreaded finding out who'll be officiating our next match. Get a run of two or three poor referees and, despite playing well, you can find yourselves five or six points worse off than you deserved.

Recently, I've played in a match where the ref booked a player for the second time and clearly forgot he'd shown a yellow to him early in the match. His own assistant trotted on, presumably to tell him he should have shown a red, but the poor guy was waved away. The player stayed on. That was in the 18th minute, thus our opponents continued with 11 on the pitch for the next 72 minutes. The consequence? Playing against ten men would have made a big difference to us in a fight to stay up.

I've seen a ref fail to give an outrageously clear offside that led to a goal against us. I'm not talking inches or even feet offside, but bloody yards. I could tell from his body language he instantly realised he'd got it wrong. But instead of maybe going through the motions of 'consulting' his assistant and then chalking it off, he stood his ground. But then lost his nerve, and players on both sides instinctively sussed this. Older lags laid into him every time he blew his whistle, and you could soon see that those who shouted and bawled the loudest got more decisions go their way. That first bad decision quickly led to another four or five.

I've been in so many matches that have been spoiled by bad officiating. So many sendings-off, penalties and free kicks that weren't. That have left us a man down or gifted goals to the opposition. I remember one match we were leading 3-2 with seconds to go. One of their attackers surged into our box and his momentum made him trip over. No one touched him, but the ref gave a penalty. Even the opposition players were looking at one another, as if to say 'is this ref for real?' But he dug his heels in and insisted it was a penalty, which was duly dispatched, and we lost two precious points in what was a major relegation battle that season. It spoils the match for everyone and, as a player, sometimes bad decisions can cost you. Relegation usually means lower wages.

So why are standards in the National leagues and below falling and what can be done about it? The refs get demoted if they're performing badly and regularly have assessors come to watch them, so you'd think the standard would be higher. It's really not. There truly are some bad ones, but they continue to be used up and down the non-leagues. And why? Because there aren't enough other referees available. So why doesn't the FA lay on more training courses to train more referees? After all, the courses they currently put on get filled up really quickly. Perhaps it's to do with the comparatively small budget that's devoted to refereeing. At the moment, it's a shade under £2m a year, which is a lot less than an average Premier League player's annual salary. That budget has to pay for the care and recruitment of 30,000 match officials in England and Wales. Without going too far into the madness of money priorities in English football generally, it's time the FA gave a much higher priority to referee training, pumped more money into the budget and laid on more training courses to get more refs into the game.

It's my strong belief that at our level we should be working towards training more and more ex-players to become referees. In cricket, it's long been the culture that ex-players become umpires. Even top players such as Paul Reiffel, Kumar Dharmasena, Ian Gould and Richard Illingworth have retrained as men in the middle. County cricket is full of them. But to my knowledge, the only ex-footballer to pick up the whistle in the last 30 years was former Huddersfield Town, Bradford City and Chesterfield player Steve Baines.

Our current crop of non-league match officials might understand the rules, but many don't understand the game because they haven't played it. Most 50-50s, for example, aren't fouls, it's just a battle for the ball. If you're going to leap for a header, your momentum will naturally take you into the opposing player and vice versa. So, often it's really not a foul. Football is a contact sport – so dur, you often have to make contact. Yes, elbows and knees do often get involved, and they can be fouls, sometimes not. But I don't see referees being able to figure out which is which on a regular basis, because they've never played the game to any decent level. I watch the decisions they make and ask myself … what have you seen there? Why did you give that? They see players clash and immediately blow the whistle. They're reactive, not anticipatory, and can't 'read' the game.

Often, refs aren't in the right place at the right time to make decisions, because they don't possess an innate positional sense. Many simply run up and down in straight lines, which means they're often obscuring a clear view of the action for themselves. I've seen referees give free kicks when it's obvious from where they're positioned that they couldn't even see the ball, never mind the tackle they'd penalised. It's alright memorising a rule book, but if you don't have the nous to know where you should be on the pitch, you're going to miss a lot and busk it.

Human error is a big part of football and I get that. As a player, I make mistakes and regularly hold my hand up and acknowledge them. So, it does my head in when individual officials resolutely refuse to admit when they've got a decision wrong. Even worse when they're cocky about it – 'I'm the ref and I make the decisions. So shut the fuck up and trot off pal.' It's hard to have respect for refs like that.

Look, I realise it's a tough and thankless job. And although I'm encouraging former players to take up the cause, sadly it would never be for me. As captain at a lot of the clubs I've played for, I've had a lot of contact with referees – and, frankly, had more than enough of them. For every decent, well-meaning ref I've dealt with before, during and after matches, my experience has been that a lot of the rest are arrogant pricks with little man syndrome. When I've been skipper, I've always made a point of seeing the ref before a match to very politely request that if there are any contentious decisions, they'll be willing to talk with me as captain and explain their reasons. A lot have agreed and stayed true to their word during the match. Just as many dismissively waved me away before the match, saying for whatever reason that their decisions are final, so you'd better suck it up.

When you see a total injustice or a plain wrong decision, that's really hard to do. I've approached so many referees of the latter kind during a match, again asking politely, 'Why did you give that free kick?' or 'How didn't you see that offside?' And the number that have imperiously waved me away and literally told me to 'fuck off' is in dozens, not single numbers. No communication, just total arrogance. Or maybe fear, because they realise inside that they've cocked up. As I've got older this has become more of a bugbear. I'm a grown-up professional sportsman and I'm respectfully querying your decision. How dare you show me so much disrespect and be verbally abusive towards me? Why should any players show you respect, when you're being such a prick?

So why haven't more players become referees? Well let's look at the process. Refereeing has a ten-tier system with, not surprisingly, the very top level being the Premier League. When you train to become a referee, you start on the bottom rung, so every current Premier League referee has at some point officiated in the National leagues and below. Thus, the average time it takes a ref to reach the top flight is 16 years. That's a massive time investment. I know the PFA has been big on trying to encourage players down this route for a while, and I've heard that some form of fast-track system for former footballers is being considered by the powers that be. I suppose all of those years of playing could count as 'foundation years', but you're still looking at a long, long 'apprenticeship', during which time you'd be earning peanuts.

Premier League and international referees can earn up to £100,000 a year and more as a full-time job. Take charge of a National League match and you won't earn far north of £100. Beneath that, after you've taken off the cost of your travel, it's pin money. The pay certainly needs improving but, to be fair, most officials outside the game have other jobs anyway. But with all the obscene amounts of money swilling around in the top tier, even if Premier League clubs committed 0.01 per cent of their collective TV money to help referees develop and increase pay for them in the lower levels, everyone would benefit. Again, it's all to do with the mad skew-whiff world of financial priorities in football. Top clubs and managers constantly complain about refereeing standards in this country yet quibble about putting more money into solving the problem, while signing yet another player on £100,000-plus a week pay.

If you had ex-pro footballers officiating, players would look at them with a bit more respect – 'He's played the game, he knows what's what.' And as an ex-player, you'd instinctively know all the little tricks that footballers use to leverage an advantage in a match. Certainly, you'd be able to read a match better than a lot of current National League refs. And, to be honest, you'd probably be a lot fitter. I know they're meant to undergo regular fitness tests, but I've been in matches where you see the ref puffing and blowing

20 minutes in, and by the latter stages of a match are that fagged out that they're regularly ten yards off the play.

My plea for recruiting more former footballers into refereeing would most positively include persuading more women who've played the game to become match officials when they finish. Mates often ask me what it's like being reffed by a woman. I couldn't care less what gender a match official is as long as they know the game and communicate well. Most female referees who've been in charge of my matches have been good and that's because I think they're still under such a dumb kind of sexist spotlight that they have to be bloody good and 'better' than a man. Hopefully, the more women who become match officials, the less of an issue that'll become.

One change I'd definitely suggest to the Referees' Association is that when they next get around to rewriting their rule book, they add a new Rule Number 1: 'Always remember, no one has come to watch you.' My heart always sinks when I watch a referee trying to become the centre of attention in a match.

So, do I think that VAR should be used in the National leagues and beyond? In its current form, not on your nelly. I've got no beef with the technology, but plenty with the way it's applied. I get it that VAR was introduced to help make for fairer football matches, and it has delivered some important turnovers that have changed the course of a match – last-ditch clearances that were already over the goal line, penalty calls that should have been made and those that shouldn't. But for me, VAR's drawbacks far outweigh its benefits.

For example, if it were to come to the National leagues my plea would be that it never be used for offside decisions. The way it's currently being applied often borders upon the ludicrous. VAR officials regularly deliver ridiculously marginal offside decisions. We've all seen so many goals chalked off because VAR has spotted the toe of a boot or part of a nose over the line. The Norwich striker Teemu Pukki had a goal disallowed because his beard was offside! To me that's not in the spirit of the game, it's not common sense and it's sucking all the joy out of football. I know the powers that be have announced that more benefit of the doubt will be given to the attacking player and that the VAR team won't intervene over 'trivial offences' but that just seems to bring in yet another level of subjectivity into the offside decision-making. What a VAR team adjudicating at one match regards as trivial or giving the benefit of the doubt might be very different from another team at a different match.

The more areas of the game that you use VAR to adjudicate in, the crazier it becomes. It breaks up the flow of a match, which is a big deal for the fans, but particularly for a footballer. The more stops and starts there are, the harder it is to get any momentum going again. Players are left in the dark for what sometimes seems like ages, while officials to-and-fro over the recordings. Much of football's appeal is that it's such a fast-moving game with relatively few disruptions.

Why is there so much gamesmanship in football? A lot of reasons, but a major one is poor refereeing, which has made it a 'game within a game' necessity. If match officials are going to 'rob' you of advantages, then as a player you'll do all that's within your power to level things up.

Gamesmanship

WHEN PEOPLE talk about football as 'the beautiful game' it glosses over the reality. At every level, players, managers and coaches work closely together day by day to do everything they possibly can to achieve one single thing – a win. Whether you're a passionate advocate of attacking football, a passing game, a more pragmatic approach or a spoiling team, we're all pursuing that same result. And whether you're Manchester City or Melchester Rovers, it takes us all down the same route into the grey area of gamesmanship.

Call it what you want. Tricks of the trade, the dark arts, a con, hoodwinking. But gamesmanship has been, and will always be, a part of football. In South America, they call it *picardia*, which means to be crafty and cunning. In life, people try to bend the rules and the laws every day and so it is in football. Is it right? Well, there are two teams on a football pitch. Who wants to win the most? Who's smart enough to be the cleverest? Or indeed, the most crafty and cunning? If it gives you an advantage, you'd be naive not to indulge in gamesmanship, particularly if poor refereeing is putting frustrating obstacles in your way. Often it can really feel like you're playing the opposition and the match officials.

It may shock some readers, but the elements of gamesmanship are literally taught to players by coaches from an early age in great detail, and more of that later. The most shocking thing to me in non-league is that a lot of young players without an academy or youth team background haven't been coached sufficiently in the art of gamesmanship. Football is often a game of fine margins, and if you don't understand what can be done to give you an advantage, it's not helping your team. Purists may not like that, but it's the reality of the game. Again, football is like life – sometimes beautiful, but often ugly and about graft and doing what you need to get by.

Let's start with the least obvious, the art of time-wasting. This may sound counter-intuitive. Most fans think they know what that means – game-managing those final minutes in a match if you're ahead or holding on to get a draw. Getting the ball into the opposition corners of the pitch and trying to stay there. Big long clearances way upfield and into the stands. Goalkeepers holding on to the ball etc. But in reality, it's much more subtle and can often start during the first few minutes of the match, depending on who you're playing.

Imagine you're away from home against a team who are on a good run, have big crowds and play on the front foot. Your scouts have told you they try to take throw-ins and free kicks as quickly as they can and hassle and harass you at pace. So, from minute one you try to slow them down, break up their game and constantly interrupt their flow. Make out you didn't understand what a whistle was for and 'innocently' kick the ball away or pass it back deep to a team-mate. Hold your hands up and shrug: 'Sorry, ref. I thought you'd given that one to us.' If you get fouled, you go down, stay down and take your time getting back up again.

Goalkeepers are key to this. They can catch the ball in the air then fall to the ground and stay there a while. They can 'dummy' their goal kicks by pretending to miscue the run-up and have to start again, spend ages looking like they're trying to 'spot' an out ball further up the pitch, and then simply roll it out to a nearby defender. Sometimes they get it agonisingly wrong. Last season, our keeper got booked after 25 minutes for time-wasting. Ten minutes from time, he got booked again for the same offence and was given a red. Not too clever. But the more you use these little spoils, the more you manage to suck time out of the match, the less time your opposition have to actually play, and the less time they have to hurt you.

Another important tactic generally in a match is to ensure the other team's best players get as little of the ball as possible. That can be achieved through totally legitimate tactics and good game management, but sometimes it requires the practice of some darker arts. As a creative midfielder I often get targeted from minute one. Recently, I played in a match where the opposition held back and allowed me far too much space. I was named man of the match, pretty much orchestrated all of our forward play and scored one plus had a couple of assists in a 5-1 win. Our next opponents obviously had a scout at the match who took a lot of notice of this. For his club's match against us they put a horrible, tough-tackling defensive midfielder on me. Within the first few minutes he was looking around to see where the ref was and, off the ball, he was raking his studs down the back of my legs, pinching me, punching me in the side. He kept this up until the ref spotted a heavy push from behind off the ball, pulled him up and gave the bloke a good talking to, his last warning. From then on, the opposition put another player on me, who also tried to kick me out of the match. As soon as the ref had a word with him, I had another player on me. They were basically rotating the players who were giving me stick, so that no one got booked or sent off. That's quite common and has happened to me throughout my career.

What all of them were looking to achieve, too, was retaliation from me. You lash out, you kick back, the ref sees that and you're off, without him having seen the earlier fouls or understood the context. I'm too old and wise to get duped into that, but I've seen plenty of players succumb to the red mist. Earlier this season, one of our young players had been giving niggle to an opposition attacker all the way through the match. Our lad went one niggle too far and, in a rage, their player literally lifted him off the ground by his hair and flung him on to the grass. That was them down to ten men.

A lot of managers positively encourage it and will tell you before a match that so-and-so sees the red mist pretty quickly, so give him stick, really wind the guy up. You might want to call that gamesmanship, but I see it as seeking out the mental weakness of an opponent. If they're a hot-head then that's a fault in their game and something they should work on. This isn't flower arranging, it's football.

'Dummying' a throw is another much-used trick and can gain you a lot of yards. You take a run-up down the line and then stop, make out as if you're looking around for a player, and then take a second run, which will take you far in advance of where you should have thrown from. It's amazing how many referees fall for it, although the good ones are usually wise to the move and wave you back with a knowing raised eyebrow.

For all my complaints about referees, they're only human and, psychologically, there are a lot of ways that footballers try to play them. The most obvious is the aggressive approach. From early in a match, some teams' game plan is to mob, intimidate and hassle the ref over every decision that doesn't go their way. Four or five players will regularly surround the poor old match official, fingers pointing, plenty of shouting, working on the basis that there's safety in numbers. The referee is hardly likely to book all five players or he'd have a riot on his hands.

I've always favoured a more subtle approach. I try to get on good terms with the ref right from the warm-up onwards, build up a rapport with him. While the opponents might be moaning and groaning at him, I'll be much more upbeat and basically butter them up. 'Well done for seeing that one, ref. Don't let them take the piss out of you today.' Or, 'I know you're clever enough to see they're taking the mickey ref, but don't let them try and get inside your head.' I talk politely and respectfully to referees all through a match. If you attack them, you just get their backs up. It's human nature – you're not going to do any favours for someone who's pissing you off. But, then again, they might do it out of fear. If you're getting continual pressure off players and their fans are on your back too, there are some referees that I've seen give in to bullying and totally buckle. They give dubious decisions and free kicks to the team that's shouting the most and the loudest.

Tactical fouls are vital tools to use for every team. You get taught by the coaches: 'The ball goes by, but the player doesn't.' You don't necessarily have to foul the guy, but if he's going to run by me, I'll take him out. How heavy the challenge is depends on where you are on the pitch and how many minutes are on the clock. If you're 15 minutes in and somewhere in the middle of the pitch, it's daft to put in a big foul. That's you on a yellow with a lot of minutes left in the match. On the edge of your box in the 91st minute when you're 1-0 up? That's a different matter. You take one for the team and accept your punishment.

High-pressing, attacking teams use tactical fouls a lot in midfield areas. They push up so many players that it leaves them susceptible to quick counter-attacks, so a defensive midfielder is usually positioned around the centre circle, ready to take out anyone who's making a run. I've watched Fernandinho at Manchester City and that's often his job and it shows in how many times he gets penalised, and sometimes booked, in that general area. De Bruyne and Sterling, talented ball players though they are, also often wade in with tactical fouls to nip a counter-attack in the bud. Manchester City rarely need to waste time because they're so often in possession, but catch them on the break and that's when you'll see how good they are at gamesmanship.

I was taught early on that if you get any contact in the opposition's box, you go down, no argument, and you'll be bollocked by the manager if you don't. Some players deliberately trail a leg so that they'll get clipped, which I'm not over-keen on. The controversial few take dives without even being touched and most players frown on that as a practice, because it's not showing any respect to your opponents. I despise divers because I think it literally jumps well over that fine line between gamesmanship and cheating. If two players are making contact in such a potentially explosive area, you both know the score and, in the end, its about who's cleverest in taking best advantage of the situation. If there's no contact at all and then there's a totally unprovoked dive, the attacker is just taking the piss. Diving and spitting continue to be the two major no-go areas for most players I know.

If it's like the Alamo in and around your own box and you get fouled, go down and stay down, take a good long breather so you can relieve the pressure on your team. Never take a throw-in straightaway. Look as if you're talking tactics with a team-mate. Drop the ball and take forever to pick it up. Ask the ref where you're meant to be taking it from. All time that's rarely taken off the watch and it's amazing how many minutes you can shave off a match.

If someone's on a booking, when they next tackle you, make a meal of it. Eleven men is better than ten. There are players who deliberately target weaker players psychologically. If someone's passing game is poor, they let them know and get inside their heads. When someone miscues a pass to a team-mate and puts it out of play, they might jog on past and say, 'This ain't going to be your day, is it pal?' They start to plant seeds of doubt and continue to work on them. Another pass goes astray, they give them a shake of the head and a sigh: 'If I'm on your side, I'd be well pissed off with you.' And another goes off-target: 'Bloody hell mate, you're having a mare. Prepare to be yanked.' I personally don't favour slagging off opposition players like that. I've had coaches who've said that football is a confidence game, so you must try to batter the other team's spirits in any way you can. I don't think that telling them how badly they're playing shows a lot of professional respect.

To help gain an advantage against teams that man-mark, at all of my clubs we've done a lot of practice into blocking off at corners and free kicks in full 11 vs 11 training matches. The aim of the game is to create space in the box by placing two of your players next to one another. One serves as the blocker, the other the runner. Both of your players will be marked, but when the ball's played in, the blocker's job is to get himself in front of your runner's marker by basically obstructing him. That gives your runner more time and space to get in a shot or header. While technically a foul, there's usually so much going on in and around the penalty area that it's hard for referees to spot. It was a tactic used constantly by England at the last World Cup, and if you rewatch their matches online, you'll see they got away with it most of the time. And that was even with VAR in operation.

The more righteous may think this is all sounds like ungentlemanly conduct. But every team does it. If you don't, you're instantly at a disadvantage. It may not be pretty, but it's the meat and potatoes side of football. For centuries, people have characterised cricket and rugby as gentlemen's sports. Really? Bouncers and sledging? The punching, nutting and holding that goes on within the scrum? Sport for all is such an important aim to enjoy and help people become fitter and get something positive into their lives. Jogging with your mates, having a cycle together, enjoying exercise classes or going to the gym – I'm a passionate advocate for all of that. But at the sharp end, ultimately the point of all genuinely competitive sports is to win matches. And as long as we have leagues, divisions, cups and competitions, it has and will always be the case.

The irony of course, is that if gamesmanship is 'happening' to your team, the fans will be up in arms and jeering and booing the 'cheats'. If your team is doing the same to the opposition, then it's all applause and shouts of 'good game management, lads!' or 'thank god we managed to get away with that one'.

Fans are notoriously one-eyed. For the English, Maradona's 'Hand of God' was a moment of despicable, cynical cheating. To Argentina's fans, it was a blessed act – the ultimate in *picardia* that helped them on their way to glory. Football will never be short of controversial talking points and drama – the top soap opera in sport. And isn't that why we love it so?

Injuries

FOOTBALL IS a contact sport and minor wear and tear is a constant reality. The club doctor and the physio become your best friends, but footballers are fit young people and tend to heal quickly from small aches, pains and strains. It's the big injuries that strike fear into the heart of any player. I can't help but feel a tremble inside when I hear of yet another player whose career has been ended by a severe injury. I was on the cusp of that and it frightened the shite out of me. Imagine being an artist and going blind. Or a musician and becoming deaf. Since being a child all I wanted to do was to play football. It was my vocation, what made sense of my life. Take that away from me and where am I?

It was an innocuous tackle halfway through the second half of a match against Stockport County. Their centre-half lunged in to rob me of the ball and our knees smashed into one another. It was a full-blooded challenge, but a fair one, fair do's to him. In most cases that kind of impact can be bloody painful, but you manage to run it off. Now and again, you can't. I tried to get up again and couldn't. Sharp pain shot through my knee and it wasn't long before the offending area had swollen up like the proverbial balloon. I couldn't bend my leg, which didn't seem hopeful. To literally add insult to injury, the Stockport fans were giving me absolute grief, convinced I was milking it to get their player sent off. Even when I was being carried away on a stretcher, they were booing and whistling. It wasn't as if I was looking for sympathy, but really? The club doctor examined me and pulled a face.

'I don't like the look of this,' he observed, not very helpfully. I was soon on my way to A&E. As we zipped across town, what immediately played upon my mind was the last major injury I'd suffered was to the same knee in my early twenties. That had kept me out for a couple of months, and it took a long while to get back into the first team. But this immediately felt a lot worse. And now I was 32 years of age and my joints had taken another ten years of battering. The knee looked all over the place and I couldn't immediately work out why. I soon discovered the reason.

After examining my knee, doing X-rays and various tests, the consultant broke, if you'll pardon the pun, the news: 'You have a stellate fracture, which means your kneecap is cracked in several places.'

'How many places?' I asked.

'Six,' he replied.

I thought on this. 'That's not good, is it?'

He shrugged and said they'd know more after they'd operated, and then added, 'But you should prepare yourself for the reality that you may not be able to play football again. We'll have to see.'

I lay in my hospital bed mulling this over. *Well screw you*, I resolved. *I'll prove you wrong and I will play again. There's no way this will stop me. I'll see everyone and anyone I need to to make this right.*

One operation later I returned home, still feeling drugged up to the eyeballs. I slept for nearly a day and then when I woke up a darker reality set in. I was wearing a heavy, uncomfortable brace on my leg, and my knee constantly ached. At the time I was single and living alone and soon discovered that being on your own with a bad injury can be demoralising. It was a painful and awkward job just to get myself up and down the stairs, never mind going to the toilet or taking a shower while wearing a full-leg, waterproof sock to protect my brace. I had to inject myself with blood thinners every day, for fear of blood clots.

My parents brought me round microwave meals because I couldn't get out to the shops. I could barely walk around my house. I couldn't drive and any kind of mobility was off the agenda. Sleep was difficult because, despite the painkillers I was on, my knee was still really painful and uncomfortable and there's nothing worse than lying awake at four in the morning, tossing and turning, fretting and worrying about your future. If I'd known at the time that I'd be out for seven months, I think I might have gone mad.

To begin with, the hardest thing was just not being able to play football. I missed the matches, the training, being with my team-mates and everything that surrounded it, particularly the camaraderie of being together. You might not be great mates, but every day you're sharing the whole player experience of being at your club. I'd always loved that, pretty much. Football has turned me into a creature of routine and when that was taken away I felt strangely lost. I'd try to get to bed and then wake up and eat my meals at the same times. But in the hours in between I'd be jittery and anxious, constantly feeling like I was late for something and should be somewhere else. I couldn't settle to anything. I made the fatal mistake of googling my injury online and scrolling through endless medical websites, always drawn to the worst-case scenarios. In the end, I had to ban myself from them.

It was when the weeks turned into months that things really started to get dark. Still with the brace on, it didn't feel as if I was making any forward progress at all. Maybe this was it? The end of my career. So, I went into denial and tried not to think about it. When the odd visitor asked how I was doing, I'd give them a cheery smile and a thumbs-up. 'Call me Arnie – I'll be back!' But in reality, I was sinking back inside myself.

I tried to lose myself in daytime TV and film DVDs, but the boredom gnaws away at you and it's hard to stay motivated for anything. Living alone is hard at times like these. When family and friends came calling, they were massive highlights to my day. I'd look out of the front window, waiting for the postman to arrive so I could hobble out to the front step just to share a few cheery morning words. I've never been a party animal, but I've always been sociable and enjoy having people around me and so often it's been around football. Being a footballer is your identity. But now you're not playing and you're asking yourself, who am I? What is it I do, apart from kick a football around? What should I be doing with the rest of my life? Long-term injuries can send you down some worrying rabbit holes.

I understand why many people might think that sports people become utterly self-obsessed with their injuries. It's not cancer or MS. It was a knee injury that might have made me rethink what I was going to do with the rest of my life. Whatever, still alive and with a lot to be thankful for. But when everything that's been important to you in your life has been so fundamentally based upon being an athlete, a physically fit specimen, this kind of problem throws you totally sideways and it caused me the most depression I've ever experienced.

Thankfully, things started to look up after a few months when the specialist told me I was ready for some physio and swimming sessions. But he remained non-committal about how successful my recovery would eventually be. It was a real lift to do proper physical activity outside of the house and to talk with people I hadn't seen for ages. But it was bittersweet to be with my team-mates. They were welcoming and full of good wishes for my return. We'd have a bit of banter about me swinging the lead and sitting on my arse all day, then they'd trot off for training, doing the things I desperately wanted to be taking part in too. What I wouldn't have given to play for ten minutes in a five-a-side match or do a skills challenge with the other guys.

I started going to the matches, because you want to show willing and support your team-mates, but really, it's the last place you want to be. A 90-minute-long reminder that you're crocked and can't play. When you know you're out injured for a lengthy spell and then get back in and around your team-mates, new and uncomfortable thoughts start to cloud your mind. *Okay, I'm full-on determined to get back. But what if I can't? What if that specialist was right? Where next?* I was 32 and knew I had at least a few more years left in me. So, although I'd been having vague thoughts about coaching and getting my badges, that had always seemed further down the line. I'd fret about this alone at home. What if it all goes tits up? I felt so unprepared for what might come next. I thought about team-mates I knew from the past whose careers ended because of anterior cruciate ligament (ACL) injuries and similar. Or nearly as bad, those who'd fought so hard to get fit and back into the game, but then had broken down again. And again. Was that going to be me? *Who'll sign me with a bad knee? How will I pay my mortgage?*

Then, because all footballers are basically selfish, I'd start worrying about the guy or guys playing in my position. I'd watch them from the stands, half hoping they'd cock up, make mistakes. Then felt crap about wishing the worst on them. I'd think about if I did return fully fit, what it would take to get back into the starting XI. *Am I to be the perennial bench man again? Will this be yet another short-term contract that won't get renewed?* So, it's shit being injured on every possible front.

My recovery wasn't without its setbacks either. Like an idiot, I went out for a walk on my crutches during a cold snap, slipped on some ice and had to stamp my foot down to save myself from going flying. The pain that reverberated up to my shattered knee was excruciating, and over the next few days I was eating strong painkillers. That put me back, as did some of the exercises I was told to do, because I totally overdid them. Essentially, I was being asked to do one very specific set of hopping exercises every day to strengthen the knee, and nothing more. But, in my wisdom, I felt strong enough to do two sessions a day, which unbeknownst to me was putting the tendon in my knee under severe and damaging pressure. I ended up getting tendonitis quite badly, which didn't help the recovery cause one little bit.

The turning point was being sent to FA headquarters at St George's for a week of intense rehab. I got to stay in the Hilton hotel they have on site and, in my case, it was all paid for by the PFA. Free food, free accommodation. Every day I was in the gym, in the pool, getting absolutely killed. Every day, all day. Even the swimming was hard work because they'd really drive you hard up and down the pool and then at intervals get you out of the water to do sets of press-ups. Then back in the water for more lengths. Then back out again for press-ups. I was pushed hard in the gym with upper-body work and stretching exercises for my legs and hips. It was rigorous to the extreme. By the end of the week, I'd lost half a stone.

I have to say the PFA are pretty amazing. Whenever I've been injured and needed surgery or rehab, they have sorted it all out for me, which makes a massive difference when you're playing at National League level. For example, the St George's rehab on my shattered knee cost £1,500 and that was all arranged and paid for by the PFA. They also provide you with a really good pension, and when you get to 35 you become eligible for a lump sum from that. If your career is finishing, there's money there to help you on to your next stage in life or next career. They're also great on health care, mental health and helping with addictions.

But in non-league, I'm one of the lucky ones. You can't join the PFA if you haven't played in the Football League. I joined the union straightaway at my first league club, and although I've turned out in non-league for the past 15 years, I retain my membership. National League players, even if they're full-time professionals, aren't eligible for membership unless they've played in the Football League.

I came back from St George's feeling rejuvenated. Not just physically but mentally. The intensity of the sessions had done me the world of good and my knee felt stronger and more flexible. But that week in rehab helped get my head back together again. For the first time in months I felt genuinely hopeful and ready to get back into the fray. St George's had taken me out of limbo land. I remembered talking to a former team-mate who'd been out for ever with an ACL and finally made his way back to playing after a year out of the game. I'd asked him what the worst part was, and his reply was almost instant. Not the initial agony, the physical hurt and pain of rehab, but the living in limbo land. Worried that you'd never make it back. The endless living in your mind, turning over the total lack of certainty, unsure what would happen next.

Now it was all about checking off little targets. Finally getting rid of the brace for good. Doing some gentle jogging. Back into the club for extra light training. Attempting some sprints. A little twisting, turning and pivoting. First, suffering pain. Then just irritating twinges. Finally, just back to normal. Being patient, building up slowly, doing as I was told. Then some training matches. Got that first challenge out of the way. The first crack on the knee. All went to plan. Except for one thing – I still hadn't made that final breakthrough. I was aware that in the training matches I kept holding back, tensing up. I realised that I was positioning my body differently, my gait was changed, turning my knee away from any potential challenge. I was protecting myself, but I knew that if I was to make a complete recovery, I had to change this safety-first mindset and throw myself fully back into the reality of the fray. But doing so was extremely scary. I'd seen so many other players come back from a long-term injury and break down at a similar point. Was I fully ready to come back? The physios all told me I was, so now it was time to get stuck in. I forced myself to go full-on in the training matches. I'd wake up the following morning, catch my breath for a second, move my leg up and down and realise with blessed relief that I was experiencing no pain. A few aches and stiffness, particularly around the knee, but no tell-tale pains.

Eventually, I made it back, but it took me a while to become a regular in the first team again. I came off the bench late in the match a few times and waited patiently until finally I was given a start. The first match back, it felt like the opening week of pre-season training. Within minutes my lungs were burning and by half-time I felt utterly knackered. You often underestimate how much a bad injury takes it out of you generally. Despite all the hard work in rehab, my muscle tone wasn't quite there, and I had a lot of graft to do building my match stamina back up again. The worst, though, was how it affected me psychologically. This wasn't a training match. It was a full-on, no-quarter-given game of football. As each tackle or challenge flew in, I imagined being cracked on the knee again and all those long, hard months of rehab being for naught. It took me a good few matches back before I stopped thinking about my knee and returned to fully playing my normal game.

The worry about injuries when you play at National League level is exacerbated by the fact that for many players, and at most clubs I've played for, you receive full pay for the first month out injured. But after that it drops to half-pay. Unfortunately, your mortgage and your bills don't. I know quite a few players who've returned to training after four weeks, knowing they were still injured, and obviously broken down again. Just so they wouldn't drop on to half their wages.

Further down the non-league pyramid, when you're basically playing for bonuses and pocket money, a serious injury is usually bad news for your actual full-time job. Not all employers are sympathetic towards part-time footballers, particularly when injuries keep them off work. I know one or two players who've actually lost their jobs as a result of getting crocked, and others who've packed in playing part-time football because they didn't want to threaten their future full-time careers, having to struggle through lengthy spells of rehab and recovery again.

What the injury did was clarify how much football meant to me. You take it for granted until there's the threat of it all being taken away. This was my life, my career. It made me realise that I wasn't ready just yet to hang up my boots and that I had a good few years left in me. In a weird kind of way, the knee injury was a big wake-up call and, once I'd returned to playing regularly again, I started to enjoy my football with a renewed passion and totally relished being back out on the pitch. It felt like I'd returned from a long, hard, miserable journey and now found myself home again. Every cloud, as they say, has a silver lining.

The Board

IN 1956, the late, great football legend Len Shackleton wrote his autobiography, *The Clown Prince of Soccer*. One chapter was entitled, 'The Average Director's Knowledge of Football' ... It consisted of a single blank page.

It's fair to say that down at Tier 8 where I currently play, non-league footballers have a much more relaxed relationship with board members at their clubs and rather more respect. At this level, as players, you'll have a drink with them after matches, they'll readily chat with you when you're in the club or when they rock up now and again to watch training. At my current side you invariably walk into the ground on matchday to find our chairman in shorts and polo shirt, working on the pitch or marking out the lines. Everyone's on first name terms and ever ready to share a joke. Our chairman never claims to be an expert on the game, but he has a lot of interesting views and opinions. Not for a second has he imposed them on the management or players but he is excited to be able to 'talk football' with people who do know the game. Most of the time he's full of questions: 'Why have you picked Joe Bloggs at right-back this week?' or 'What's the reason for us playing 4-1-3-2 today?' He's always interested to know why what he calls 'the football people' make the decisions they do. He never claims to 'know' football, because he's a fan and one of the people who keeps the club running. There's no status thing with him at all. That's my kind of chairman.

Even at my previous club in Tier 6, the chairman was totally approachable. He used to come on the coach with us to matches and play cards with players at the back of the bus. There were two other directors there who I'd regularly team up with to play golf. There was a real sense of 'we're all in this together'. I know down at Lewes FC their chairman writes the programme notes, manages their website and deals with all the press and media. Up and down the country, board members man the turnstiles, sell the programmes and pull pints in the clubhouse.

The higher up the pyramid you go, the more distant owners and boards tend to be from their players, staff and fans. At all the former Football League clubs I've played for in the National League, the chairmen would turn up in their Bentleys and Jags in club suits and ties and you were very aware it was us and them. You definitely weren't on first name terms. It was all very deferential. 'Good morning Mr Chairman,' and 'How are you, Mr Chairman?' They were the big bad bosses and you were the staff. God forbid you'd ever see any of them pitching in to help around the ground. That's for the peasants.

Usually, my personal encounters with big-club chairmen ended unhappily. At one of those former Football League clubs, I and some of the other players were summoned to the boardroom after training one day. We were all worried because it was so unprecedented to be called into the inner sanctum. One of the directors sat us down and told us that they'd whittled their search for a new manager down to two candidates. As we'd all played for one or either of them, he wanted our confidential, honest opinions on both. One of the two managers had completely frozen me out at a previous club and, in my opinion, which I freely gave, he was a nightmare to work with. I guaranteed the director that if he was appointed I'd be on my way. There's no way he'd keep me at the club. At the time I was playing really well and had racked up a string of man-of-the-match performances, so I could tell the director was taking notice of what I said. I also suspected the director was worried about the idea of players being shipped out en masse and being replaced by higher wage earners.

In the end, the other candidate was chosen. But, somehow, what had been said at this so-called 'confidential' meeting got back very soon afterwards to the losing candidate's regular assistant, who also happened to share my agent. My agent rang me up and gave me a total slagging off. How dare I bad-mouth good, experienced managers to board members? But I thought, *Bollocks to this. I'm not carrying the can*, so I just downright lied and told my agent I had no idea what he was talking about. I knew my other team-mates hadn't passed anything on from the meeting, so that just left our club director. Shitbag.

The only times you'd ever see a chairman appear in the dressing room at clubs like that, you knew you were in for some form of bollocking. It was always after a defeat and, as he came through the door, you could see that everyone was shitting themselves. At one of my clubs, the chairman stormed into our inner sanctum and screamed a mighty hail of abuse, telling us what useless little shits we all were, and then gave us a lot of threatening talk about cancelling contracts and freezing certain players out. We were killing the club and unless we pulled our fingers out he'd personally pass on what lazy little bastards we were to any future employers. If relegation was on the cards, it wasn't only the club that was going to suffer.

At another of my clubs, we were in the changing room after one match, just having lost away down in Essex, hardly a massacre, a one-nil defeat. It had been an overnight hotel stay as we were so far away. We were all pissed off and nothing much was being said, everyone preparing themselves for a long, deflated drive back north on the coach. Suddenly the dressing room door opens and in comes the chairman with one of the other directors in tow. It was rare for directors to come in to see us after a match and, from the look on the chairman's face, this wasn't going to be good news. He kept it fairly calm.

If we didn't get our act together, we were going down. And that would have a massive impact on the club. And on us guys. Wages and bonuses all get cut. A lot of us wouldn't be seeing new contracts. He was firm but calm. There was an awkward pregnant silence. I for one, and as one of the more senior players at the club, just didn't know how to respond. The silence seemed to go on forever. And then the other director totally went off on one. Total full-on rage. He was effing and blinding at us all.

'You don't fucking care. None of you give a shit about this club. You're not trying.'

Our captain, who was a decent lad, wasn't having the 'not trying' jibe and went for him. 'How the fuck can you say that?'

So, the director went for him. Totally went for him. Slapping and punching, there was froth coming out of his mouth. And what you have to bear in mind is that we all pretty much knew this guy, and he was usually quite posh and well-spoken. But now he was going berserk. We couldn't believe the words that were coming out of his mouth. The two of them had to be pulled apart. He and the chairman left and, after the door was closed, there was a long silence. Then someone made a daft comment and everybody burst out laughing. But everyone in that room knew there were dark clouds on the horizon for us all. As I say, it's rare that members of the board come into the changing rooms straight after a match.

It probably sounds childish, but when we were on the coach back up the motorway, the chairman and the director passed us in their car. There was quite a lot of booing and jeering and middle fingers flying up in the air after they passed us. Later that week, the captain and the director were forced to meet up and formally apologise to one another. But it still stuck in my craw. As a professional, the one thing you never accuse a footballer of is not trying. We all have bad matches, times when our confidence isn't high, so we play safe. We have matches we make mistakes in. There are some not very good players who screw things up because they can't achieve better. But to say a lad isn't trying is a smack in the mouth.

In my experience, the more fiercely ambitious a board or owner is, the quicker their relationship with players and fans disintegrates. This must sound counter-intuitive. Don't all fans want success? Well, yes – but not at all costs. What I've experienced is that the further the fans feel from the people who run their club, over time they become less committed, less interested. More money to spend! Serious ambition to go up a few leagues! Who wouldn't want it? Well, it all comes with a price.

Most players don't care where the money is coming from, they just want to know there is some. To be fair, when I've played at clubs that have rich owners, I've always appreciated that they're subsidising my wages and helping the club be more competitive.

So, you get a new owner or board who have mega ideas about revolutionising your club. Fantastic! The first season or so is a dream. You get the likes of steel magnate and football-mad benefactor Glenn Tamplin, who took over at Billericay Town while they were in the National South. His ambition was to rise the leagues and get Billericay into the EFL. For a couple of seasons, the club were signing, by non-league standards, incredibly expensive ex-top league players approaching the end of their careers. Former Spurs and Wolves player Jamie O'Hara was allegedly on four grand a week, playing in the sixth division.

I don't know what's happening inside Billericay Town right now, but from the outside it seems that he left them in a better place. Their ground looks much improved, but there's no time soon that Billericay Town are going to be signing players on two or three grand a week again. They're still in the National South, which is where they started when Glenn Tamplin took over.

Beckham, the Neville brothers et al., plus the billionaire businessman Peter Lim have bankrolled Salford City from the Northern Premier into League Two. Okay, they've achieved a lot, invested a lot of money into the playing staff, the ground and the infrastructure. All good for Salford City. There's a sense here that because of the owners' money and who they are, they'll attract a lot more sponsorship dosh. Therefore, the reliance on money from fans turning up to matches becomes less important.

I've no gripe with Salford about what they've done to make matchdays a much better experience for fans. They clearly have, and good on them. But in League Two, they're regularly pulling in fewer fans than when they were in the National League in 2018/19. Salford is a city that has a population of over 100,000 and is in Greater Manchester, a conurbation with 2.8 million living on their doorstep. Okay, they have Manchester United and Manchester City up the road, but so do Stockport County in the National League, who currently pull nearly three times Salford's average home gate. Salford's fellow League Two team Oldham Athletic double that. So, what's stopping more local football fans going to watch Salford every week? Is it because their star-studded celebrity board are so far from the fans that they may as well be a Prem club in miniature?

Nonetheless, Salford, like Forest Green Rovers, have made it into the Football League. But for every success story, there are a legion of sad tales about Billy Bigwallets who took over clubs that no longer exist or have been bankrupted and forced to rise from the ashes much further down the pyramid. George Reynolds's reign of madness at Darlington now has them sharing a ground with the local rugby club. They're still running, but other clubs haven't been so lucky.

Non-league football clubs are constantly on the look-out for investors. Or should I say donors? Because if anyone who puts money into a club is expecting a return on their 'investment', they're living in cloud cuckoo land. It's a money pit out there. As the old joke goes, it's easy to make a small fortune running a non-league football club. First, start with a large fortune ...

Even success comes at a cost. Get promoted into the National League and your ground has to live up to some exacting standards. It must have a minimum capacity of 4,000, with the potential to achieve a capacity of 5,000 in the future, and have a covered area containing a minimum of 500 seats. The club must be able to segregate home and away fans and any segregated areas should have separate entrances, exits, toilets and catering facilities. Each ground must also have changing areas that are at least 18 square metres in size, excluding the showers and toilets. The ground must also have a permanent TV gantry exactly on the halfway line and at least four metres tall. As a consequence, for some clubs promotion has involved a lot of building work and improvements and none of that comes cheap. All money that the board has to find from somewhere. Rather like referees, I'm really not sure why anyone would want to be a board member, but I'm very glad they do. Without a board, there's no football club.

Agents

I'VE ONLY ever had two agents. The first picked me up in the reserves at the League One club I started out at. He had a few other players there and made contact with me through one of his first-team regulars. My dad and I were invited around to his house.

I was dead keen, but as usual Dad was the voice of caution and said let's hear what he has to say first before we get ahead of ourselves.

He was very flash and boasted about some of the players and managers he represented. It certainly impressed me – Scholes, Verón, Gareth Southgate and Big Sam. But essentially, and my dad finally agreed, he seemed to be a decent guy. The agent said he'd get me a boot deal, which he did with Umbro. I was 17 and, every month or so from then on, boxes of top-of-the-range boots would arrive for me at the club. What could possibly go wrong?

To my utter shock, my dear old League One club released me. But hey, no problem. I had an agent now. He'd find something for me. A League Two team in the Midlands were interested, but my agent nearly kiboshed the deal by asking them for £5,000 for negotiating on my behalf. They told him they didn't pay agents' fees, so I decided that he and I should part ways.

I did really well at my new club and soon attracted the attention of an agent who'd been a former player and impressed me with his knowledge of the game and his understanding of what players needed in terms of support and security. He was totally kosher, FIFA-licensed and seemed a great fit for me. His deal was 2 per cent of my gross salary. He got me an accountant and a mobile phone as part of the deal and put me in touch with a mate of his who did amazing deals on concerts and gig tickets, so I was well pleased.

We stayed together throughout my entire professional career in the National leagues. I tended to go to clubs where my agent already had contacts and he did manage to get me better wages wherever I went. If I'd been a centre-forward who scored 25 goals a season, I wouldn't have needed an agent, but I'm a midfielder and he 'sold' me far better than I could have, on or off the pitch. He represented a lot of players in much higher leagues who he'd have to do brand and sponsorship deals for, but I was very low maintenance. We only really needed to talk when I was ready to move on to a new club or renegotiate a contract at my current one. But it was good to know there was always someone there who was batting on your behalf. An agent can also act as a buffer between you and the club, which is sometimes very useful.

After a good few years together, we eventually parted amicably when I went semi-pro – I didn't really need him anymore from then onwards. The further down the pyramid you go, the smaller and tighter the budgets and an agent doesn't get much chance to barter up wages at those levels.

Is it important for a non-league player to have an agent? If you're young and ambitious and want to progress your career up a league or two, then definitely 'yes'. A good agent can get you through doors that can remain closed if you're trying to represent yourself. Also, what young player understands the ins and outs of contracts or the legal sides of signing on for a football club? Additionally, when you try to rep yourself as a young player, clubs aren't stupid. Most young players are desperate to get a contract, so when the chair says they can't possibly pay any more than, say, £400 a week, they're generally very reluctant to argue for more. An agent has done that for me several times and got much more than the 'figure' the club claimed was their absolute ceiling. But first, a word of warning – there are a lot of cowboys out there.

A few years ago, FIFA basically deregulated the rules on agents. Previously, any would-be agent had to sit a famously tough entrance exam, take out indemnity insurance and have a detailed understanding of contract law. But FIFA found it impossible to police the thousands of transfers that were going on around the world, so they handed the responsibility over to individual FAs. So, currently in England and Wales, it's a doddle to register as an agent as long as you don't have a criminal record, aren't bankrupt and have £500 to give the FA to sign up. There's no longer an exam or any qualification that agents have to work towards so, basically, any old Joe Shmoh can register with the FA, irrespective of what knowledge or experience in the field they may or may not have.

Before the deregulation, there were just over 500 registered agents in the world – now there are tens of thousands. So, not surprisingly, in this country alone we have a good few who are bloody useless and incompetent, plus some who are likely to rip you off. These days agents generally receive between 4 and 10 per cent of a player's contract. I know a young player who was persuaded to sign over 20 per cent to his new agent. A total rip-off. One club I was at, one of our young players was approached by an agent who turned out to be a total cowboy. The guy asked him for £250 to make a video of him in training. A lot of people are suspicious of showreels of actual match highlights, so what use is footage of a player training? A total waste of time for the kid and, ultimately, a waste of £250.

These days, young non-league players need to be really careful if they're approached by an agent wanting to represent them. Look first at their track record and who else is on their books. Do they represent any big hitters or any other footballers you know personally? If the latter, give them a ring and ask how they're finding life with their agent. Ask around and do your own due diligence before you even think about putting pen to paper.

The greater majority of agents genuinely have their players' well-being at heart. It's what pays their mortgages, and most are scrupulous about protecting their reputations. In my experience, the best agents are also genuine football fans. Top operator Paul Stretford is the perfect example. Not only does he represent the likes of Wayne Rooney and Harry Maguire, through his company Triple S Sports and Entertainment Group, he also owns current FA Vase holders Warrington Rylands. The club is in his family's blood and, after starting off as a sponsor, he also helped them out financially during some difficult spells. In 2019, he took things one step further and became their owner.

The National leagues are an important hunting ground for bona fide agents. The reality of the current situation is that players are being offered shorter and shorter contracts at the top end of non-league. If an agent has several National League players on their books, they're going to be kept busy negotiating new contracts or renegotiating old ones. It won't earn the agency a fortune but is good, regular bread and butter money.

Where the holy grail for agents lies is in finding the next Jamie Vardy or Charlie Austin. Discover a diamond early in their careers and you have a player who'll keep on giving. If they're real quality, they'll be moving upwards and onwards with some regularity. Each time they rise higher, the agent gets a lucrative percentage of bigger and better wages plus a cut of transfers. Get them into the Championship on a good deal, and the agent's on a serious earner. Get them into the Premier League and it's quids in. Even a player from non-league who makes it into regular League One or League Two football can turn a handy little profit for their agent with regular moves.

A decent agent is never going to ask you for anything up front. The greater majority of them make a damn good living. At the top level, agents do all the legwork buying houses, overseas holiday properties and cars for their clients. They sort out their holidays, home security, gardening and domestic help. Some even provide daily VIP catering for their players. None of that comes cheap and the top agents are very wealthy men.

I got first-hand proof of that at one of my former clubs. A major agent lived nearby. The guy's house was massive, and in the grounds there was a floodlit 4G pitch. His son was a young player at a league academy and his dad wanted him out on loan to get some competitive match time. He struck a deal with my club, who not only got his lad for free, but also use of his training pitch. For the next few months, two or three times a week, there'd be 20 or so cars parked up his long and very impressive driveway, while we got stuck into training with some of the best facilities we'd ever enjoyed.

To put the cream on the cake, the agent also let us use his games room, complete with bar and Sky Sports on a big screen, to chill out in after training. A few of us looked around this amazing house and manicured grounds and wondered what the hell we were doing playing football? We should set up as agents, if this was any reflection of how much you could earn.

And then we all remembered why not. We hadn't got a clue about the intricacies of contract law, finance and negotiation techniques, let alone knew enough footballers who had any trade value.

He was agent for a lot of big names, and one evening he asked Neil Warnock along to give us a motivational speech, which was truly inspiring. Warnock has been around the game for many decades and it was clear why he still remained in football. He was still like a kid kicking a football around, full of positivity and enthusiasm. It was a joy to be in the room that night.

Inevitably the day arrived when the agent's son finished his loan spell with us. He was a good kid, but I must admit we missed his dad more. No more luxury under a floodlit pitch, no more games room R&R, but it was good while it lasted.

There's been much debate about agents and all the money they take out of the game, and I understand it. At the top level it seems obscene that one individual can be leveraging tens of millions for themselves out of a single player deal. But further down the tree I'd still recommend young players to find a decent agent if they can. As a footballer you might be part of a team at the moment, but throughout the life of your career, you're flying solo. Unless you have an agent. Family and friends are brilliant at giving emotional support, but they know nothing about the nuts and bolts of contracts and life inside football generally. And neither do most young footballers.

There's sometimes this quaint view of non-league as being this romantic ideal of football at its purest, playing football for football's sake. A jolly little world of groundhoppers, ever-smiling fans, hand-made pies and real ale. The fuller reality is a little different. Non-league clubs have to be ruthless and hard-headed. Living, or more often surviving, on tight budgets and financial uncertainty, they're not surprisingly going to offer young players the very least they can. It's agents, knowing what the score is, who manage to get young players a bit more money and better and longer contracts. And in a world of increasing 'contract churn' where older players are lucky to get one-year deals, they're invaluable in keeping clients in work and in the game.

The Media

I ENJOY talking about football. I like explaining myself and what I think. So I've always been okay about dealing with the media. It's a joy these days to see non-league football getting so much more exposure. When I first started out, you'd get match reports in your local newspaper and that was about it. The only times it got wider coverage was on FA Cup days when non-league clubs were playing Football League opposition and then the narrative was always the same. Plucky little minnows take on the big boys, add further tired old clichés and repeat.

But with the rise in importance of social media, the ball game has changed completely. Match reports, interviews and even highlights are online within hours of a game finishing. But I still have to give a big shout-out to the old traditional print media who cover and support non-league football through thick and thin.

At every club I've been at, there has been a local newspaper, usually a weekly, that's covered the team for aeons and tend to have a good ongoing relationship with their clubs. In the main, local reporters are also fans of the team and, although they don't pull any punches when things are going badly on or off the pitch, there's an intimate understanding there about how the club operates. Yes, it's a local sports reporter's job to 'get the story' but they also have to balance this with their relationship with the club. Of course, there are times when clubs need to keep things under wraps with certain issues. For example, it wouldn't help a club's image with its fans if they were to know about every training ground bust-up and every player fall-out that goes on. Football can become an emotional game and tempers can quickly fray when tackles are being thrown in at training. So there has to be some give and take between local reporters and their clubs.

What I can't take is journalists trying to make a name for themselves by continually hitting the controversy button. One club I played for had a reporter whose main job was to cover our team for the local newspaper, and he was brutal. We'd win a match, and his match report would be a long litany of criticism about how we should have won by more, were lucky, didn't really deserve to get our three valuable points. His man of the match would get ratings of five or six, the rest one, two, three and four. There seemed to be such a bitterness and negativity about his attitude towards the club and, as players, we couldn't work out why. Was he trying to be a controversialist to further his own career? Or just an arrogant young sod who had a little too much self-importance?

Mostly, we just laughed at his attitude. His match reports showed little understanding of football, its tactics and how it should be played. But it was hard to laugh in the end, because this particular club had a set of very negative fans who were always on our backs as players. What he increasingly did was throw fuel on the fire and whip up the fans to be even more vocally harsh and abusive. I don't know what became of him and don't really care. Whether he knew it or not, his coverage served to make life a lot harder for players at that club. Words have consequences.

When I look at the runaround top players are given by the national red tops, I feel relieved to be down here in non-league football. They're continually under the microscope in everything they do and everywhere they go. I couldn't bear that kind of attention. It's nothing to do with playing football but says a lot about the celebrity culture that now surrounds the game at the highest levels. The reporters have no interest in football, only in the lurid and the kiss and tell. I don't care how much you earn, it must be crap to have paparazzi camped on your doorstep and outside every restaurant and social event you attend.

I always try to be honest and straight up when I'm being interviewed, particularly during the times when I've been the club captain. Over the years I think I've gained a lot of respect from the press for trying to give them the full picture, even if some of it has to be off the record. I've told them, 'Look, I can give you some information or some further context so you understand what's going on behind the scenes, but it can't go in the paper.' Journalists have always respected that, because once they get to know me, they understand I don't give them any bullshit. I think they also realise that if they did let me down, I wouldn't be anywhere near as open about things in the future. It's a two-way street.

In terms of what happens on matchday, I'm a big believer in owning it when you've screwed up. Recently my club were playing away at a fairly mediocre northern club and got battered 4-0. I did an interview for a YouTube channel straight after the match and I told it like it was: 'No excuses, we were terrible out there. From back to front, we were pathetic today.' Then I tried to analyse why as honestly as I could. After we'd recorded the interview, the journalist gave me an amazed look. 'You don't hold back, do you?' he said.

'Nine times out of ten, I interview players after a match like that and they're full of excuses, blame the ref, the opposition, anyone but themselves. That was refreshing.'

The fact is it's an insult to everyone's intelligence to make excuses for a poor performance. The fans and the press all see it with their own eyes and, as footballers, you all know when you've played a bad game. Managers are the worst, but I suppose most of them are perennially only a few matches away from the sack so need to cover their backs as best they can.

Whatever any footballer tries to tell you, everyone makes sure they get a peek at their match ratings in the press. You know yourself whether you've played well, badly or totally indifferently, but what you really want to see is what other people think. There are reporters at certain papers whose opinions I trust and to get a 5 from them when you thought you'd played a 7 doesn't exactly spoil your Saturday night, but it does rankle. You're always being judged as a footballer – by the manager, the fans, other players. But a bald number is at the sharp end of judgements.

You get to know when some reporters are tougher than others with their marking, so take it accordingly. Sometimes though, it piddles you off, because often fans and reporters don't spot the little things that you may do as a player that all helps towards swinging a match. A run you made to deliberately draw out a defender, so your forwards had more space to work in. Or how you held up the ball to give your very out-of-position team-mates the time to get themselves organised. It's these little footballing moments that often lead to the big ones. When football reporters pick up on what's happening underneath the more obvious action, that's when I have respect for their analysis.

Just as I think more footballers should become referees, I also reckon that it's an absolute positive when former players go into the media and become football journalists. I'm not talking here about becoming a summariser or pundit for radio or TV, I mean honest-to-goodness match reporting. Retired footballers have spent virtually all their lives in the game and know it inside out. They can also spot the more subtle elements of play that a lot of reporters may not. It's encouraging to see that half a dozen universities in this country are now offering sports reporting degrees. Derby University recently became the first to offer a specific BA (Hons) in Football Journalism.

Nationally, the weekly bible of non-league football is the *Non-League Paper*. For the uninitiated, it carries news features, match reports, plus player and staff interviews. It's flown the flag for non-league for over 20 years now and comes out on a Sunday, so it contains Saturday's match reports and results. Over the summer close season there are more in-depth features and discussion pieces, which I find fascinating. It's interesting to read what other personalities in non-league are thinking about the issues that affect our game, and the *Non-League Paper* is one of the few truly national forums for that. My dad has been buying it since day one.

It was thanks to the *Non-League Paper* that I once got a good ribbing from my team-mates. They printed a feature interview with me but used the wrong photo. There's a player in non-league who's pretty much my doppelganger and they'd incorrectly used his picture with the piece. An understandable mistake, but for weeks afterwards nobody in the squad called me by my proper name but by his. I felt like Rodney always being called Dave by Trigger in *Only Fools and Horses*.

A big shout-out should also go the brilliant *Non-League Football Show*. Created in 2006 by leading sports journalist and former Chelmsford City director and CEO Caroline Barker, it started life on BBC London, then went national on BBC Radio 5 and is now a very popular independent podcast. For years, it's been a must listen to for players, fans and, well, anyone involved with non-league football. Full of stories and debate, I've always loved listening – and on a couple of occasions taking part in the chat. Like the *Non-League Paper*, it's been an important media outlet that's championed the world I live in without being in any way sycophantic. For me, both have worked hard to be supportive but always unafraid to criticise when needed, and to condemn when their passion has become clear. I think that more than any other news sources they both do a great job of recording and reflecting upon the reality of life in non-league. My strong suspicion is it's because they very much care about it.

My dad has a collection of newspapers, magazines, videos, radio recordings and DVDs of me going right back to my under-10s days, with virtually everything that's ever been written about me, interviews I've done and clips of my performances. One day, probably when I've retired, I'll sit down with him and go through everything on a trip down memory lane. But, right now, there are still more column inches to be filled and clips to be filmed. There's life in the old dog yet.

Now, of course, with social media, clubs don't have to wait for the press and broadcasters to toddle along and give them coverage. They can do it themselves. Despite being in Tier 8, my own current club has a healthy presence on Facebook and Twitter, and clips from our matches are regularly downloaded on to YouTube.

At Tier 7, you have the social media success story of FC United of Manchester. They're followed on Facebook by 850,000 people around the world. On Twitter, the club has 85,000 followers. That's a lot of online fans, and as FC United are a fan-owned club, it wouldn't be surprising if several of those online supporters are chipping in money to help them too. There are other knock-on effects. Their social media platforms also prominently advertise their merchandise and souvenirs – massive shop windows. The kind of numbers that follow them are of big interest to potential sponsors as well. Effectively, social media is helping FC United become a 'cult' club around the world. And that's in the seventh tier of English football.

Then there's Dulwich Hamlet, famous for their ultras and social campaigning. On Twitter they're followed by 30,000 people around the globe, 13,000 on Instagram, and 9,000 on Facebook. Not quite FC United figures, but still impressive for a Southern League South club. That's many, many times their average home gate of around 2,000, and the club's impressive website and their own television channel, Dulwich Hamlet TV, is drawing ever more fans from around the world.

So, gone are the days when non-league clubs were purely 'local'. Social media has helped them reach out to a much wider world of fans who are thirsting for something more genuine and down-to-earth than the corporate, sterile, money-grabbing top leagues around the globe. Who knows, but right now there may well be people walking around Moscow, Madrid and Minnesota proudly wearing their FC United and Dulwich Hamlet shirts. That would have been unthinkable a few years ago, unless they were expats.

As we know, though, social media can also prove to be a major source of embarrassment. A few years ago, the club I was at thought it would be a good idea to make a special players' feature and put it up on YouTube for the fans to enjoy. Face to camera, I and the rest of the players were individually asked questions such as: 'Who's the worst-dressed player in the squad?' 'Who's got the crappest car?' 'Who'd be your favourite dinner guests?' – that kind of thing. It was meant to be light and a bit of a laugh but, in truth, it turned out as the most cheesy, cringeworthy thing I've ever done. It was appalling. We were given the questions on the spur of the moment and had no time to think about our answers. So, I 'ummed and erred' my way through long silences and hopelessly inarticulate replies and frankly just embarrassed myself. But, believe me, I wasn't the worst by a long chalk. Some of the lads were so lost for words that they just stared at the camera and shrugged, while everyone else laughed in the background.

The worst was that it was put up on YouTube as raw, unedited footage, which made us all look really dumb. The comments section wasn't kind to us. But it taught me an important lesson. If you get asked to do an interview or a feature, make sure you're prepared and that you've done your homework. Otherwise, you've got no one to blame but yourself if you come off looking like a complete dork. Top players often receive coaching in how to deal with the media and advice on what to say – and not say! – in interviews. In non-league, there's no such luxury. The worst, of course, is that my sad little YouTube feature is still up there and will be for years to come!

I do think that a lot of clubs could do more with their online efforts in the future. It's the perfect way to connect with fans in a positive way and let the 'personality' of the club come through. This might sound mad, but one idea that could be a lot of fun would be filming an ongoing mini-golf competition between the players and staff throughout a season. Have a leader board, regular videos of great and awful shots, fluffs, laughs and out-takes. Or around Christmas time, you could create an online 'advent calendar', where for each day an individual player at the club talks about what presents they'd like or how they'll be spending the day, whatever.

These types of feature offer a snapshot into what the players and staff are like when they're not on the pitch or the touchline. Daft little things like this give fans another little connection with their club and it's just the sort of thing that could counterbalance the more corrosive stuff on social media. Portray us as people who fans can relate to on a human level rather than punch bags to be furiously slagged off when results aren't going our way. One thing's for sure: if you seek publicity and want more coverage for your club, your league, then you have to take the rough with the smooth, because sometimes shit happens.

Betting and Bribes

THERE'S A silent epidemic out there in football and it's been around for decades. The betting culture is endemic in the game. Most of us will have heard about the struggle that top players such as Paul Merson and Tony Adams have had with gambling – and why Adams set up his Sporting Chance clinic to help fellow players. But the problem cascades deep down into non-league too. The tragic joke of this is that a legion of betting companies now sponsor individual clubs – and an army of footballers spend their spare time giving them their money back.

I've no idea how betting works, so I've always kept away from it, but every club I've been at has had a really heavy betting culture in the dressing room. Dogs, horses, golf, tennis, who was going to walk through the dressing room door next, anything. A lot of players – and I mean a lot – spend way more on betting than they can realistically afford. One lad at my last club was sweating on a £500 bet he had on a horse and that was more than he earned in a week. That was crazy, high-risk gambling – not to place but to win. It was clear from the tenners he tried to borrow off everyone the following week that the horse hadn't come home for him. And they only tell you when they've won a bet, never about the many times they lost.

The rules have changed over the years. When I first started out, you weren't allowed to bet on your own club or any other club in your division. Then it broadened out and you couldn't bet on any club in the UK. I remember team-mates betting on Hungarian Division 2 matches that they knew nothing about or staying up until five in the morning to watch Australian matches they had money on.

Now players aren't allowed to bet on football, full stop. Or pass on any information they have, such as team selection or injury news, to family, friends or associates. Not that it stops them. Only recently, two Boston United players were banned and fined by the FA for placing over 750 bets between them on football matches over a five-year period. Andi Thanoji was handed a five-month ban and fined £950; Jay Rollins, a one-month ban and a £500 fine. They were more blatant, but I know a lot of players who put bets on through friends, partners, brothers and sisters.

The rules might change, but the dressing room betting just moves somewhere else. And, in truth, it must be damned hard to police. A few years ago, Rushden & Diamonds had massive money troubles. All their players upped and left because they hadn't been paid. So, word went round that Rushden would be putting out their youth team for their next match the coming Saturday. Most of the players at my club lumped a fortune on them to lose, through third parties, and of course Rushden got battered. I think there was an investigation once word got out, but I don't know anyone that was charged with anything from my old club or any other.

I had a manager with a bad gambling problem. It's not a good look when you're trying to retain players' respect, to constantly try to cadge money off your staff. It's still a massive issue in non-league football. Some of them are quite literally spending their mortgage money on bets and getting into deep financial trouble.

Even on player nights out, ending up in a nightclub was never enough for the gamblers. At two or three in the morning, while the majority of us were wending our way home, the hardcore would be off to a casino until the following morning, invariably losing a fortune in the process. I used to ask them whether they'd ever seen a poor casino owner or an impoverished bookie. Of course not. It's them making the money, not the poor mugs who fill their tills.

Online betting has made the problem worse. Wherever you are, whatever you're doing, as long as you have your smartphone, you can lay some bets. I've often seen players in the dressing room before matches, phones out, placing money on something or other. Football is a competitive game, full of competitive people, and I've watched players sitting there trying to outdo one another on how much they're spending online on their betting apps.

But it can be a quick and slippery slope into addiction. The story of Scott Davies is one that should serve as a warning to any players who think it's easy to kick the betting habit. Scott's played for several non-league clubs, including Aldershot, Wealdstone and Slough, over the years. But he started off at Reading in the Premier League and by his late twenties was suicidal and playing in the Southern League. Scott reckons he's lost over £200,000 to his gambling addiction, a good chunk of that while on a non-league player's wages.

As a teenager he'd already begun having a flutter at the bookies, but it was while out on loan to Aldershot in the Conference that his addiction really kicked in. He started to play poker on the team bus and ended up owing £2,500 to a team-mate. Scott's mum and dad bailed him out of that problem, but the shame of that didn't stop him. He stayed at Aldershot for a further season and spent all his wages on betting within four or five days of each payday.

He tells stories of blowing £30,000 that was meant to be a deposit on a house. His frantic parents took his bank cards away from him – so he got himself some credit cards and soon maxed those out. Before he sought help, Scott reckons he was gambling away 80 to 90 per cent of his wages. Over the years, he borrowed and lost huge amounts of money from his family and got himself into mountains of debt. Things got so bad that his former footballer father packed his son's bag in an act of tough love and told him to leave the family home and learn how to look after himself properly.

A sad thing for me is that Scott was a really talented footballer, who ended up putting gambling before his career. At his worst, he spent every waking day thinking first about what bets he'd lay and only then about playing football. Thankfully for Scott, who's a really thoughtful and articulate guy, he eventually got help from the Sporting Chance clinic and now helps to educate sportspeople about the risks of gambling addiction problems. Hopefully, his experiences are helping players pull back from the brink and reassess their gambling problems. But my current experience continues to be the same: lots of players in my dressing room who waste more than they should on betting and, of course, usually losing their hard-earned money.

So why is there such a silent epidemic? Sometimes, I wonder how much of it's down to boredom. As a footballer, there's a lot of waiting around – for matchday to arrive, long hours spent on coaches, all those in-between hours when you're not training or playing or getting that adrenalin rush that football gives you. I suppose betting offers an instant hit.

There's a lot of peer pressure in football. Younger players try to imitate the older players because they want to be seen as one of the 'gang'. And many lads also feel a pressure to live up to a certain kind of flashy footballer image. When you look from the outside, it must seem daft. These are non-league players on hundreds a week if they're lucky, not tens of thousands. But being a footballer can be very seductive. You might only play in front of a thousand or so fans every week down in Tier 5 or 6, but you're in the public spotlight. You're a somebody. You get your name in the papers and your match highlights on YouTube. You want to look like you're 'living the life', and the dressing room betting culture is often a big part of that. But bravado can come at a costly price.

The bottom line for me is that the powers that be don't have any great appetite for clamping down further on this, because betting companies funnel so much money into English football. They can point to the rules they've brought in for players and betting, but it's clearly not working.

The truth is, betting amongst footballers has a long history; it's nothing new. Back in the 1960s, Sheffield Wednesday players Peter Swan, Tony Kay and David Layne were all famously found guilty of betting on their own team to lose. The trio all received short prison sentences and bans from football in a scandal that shocked the nation. Criminal prosecutions for inter-team match-fixing go back even further.

Can you imagine the players at Manchester United and Liverpool of today colluding to fix a match? Seven of them did back in 1915 and got themselves banned for life from football. Relegation-threatened Man U had to win the match to stay up. Three United players plotted with four of their Liverpool opponents to throw the match. United won

2-0. But greed got to them all in the end. A large amount of money was put on the match at odds of 7/1 on a 2-0 United win and all traced back to the players.

Does match-fixing happen today in non-league football? The nearest I came to it was on the final day of the season some years ago. My club were solidly mid-table with nothing much to play for and we were playing a team who were desperate to go up. Their task was simple – they had to win the match. In truth, they were nailed-on favourites before the match began. We were an okay team, but they were superior in all departments. Our manager was really good mates with the boss of the promotion hopefuls and told the guy he'd rest some of our regulars for the match. It wasn't for money, but because someone knew someone, we didn't try over-hard. They won and clinched promotion.

We discovered afterwards that our physio room was full of crates of beer, plates of food and bags of snacks, presumably all courtesy of you know who. None of us knew it would be waiting for us there, and if that was a bribe, it was a pretty sorry one.

Was it wrong to do? Who knows? Has a similar thing happened before or since? Probably yes. We didn't throw the match in any way and I can honestly say I just played my normal game and performed pretty well. But the truth is that if you've got nothing left to play for in your final match of the season, your foot's generally off the gas anyway and you're thinking about your summer holidays. The opposition were so up for it anyway that they'd have won, no doubt. But the beers and grub were a nice, unexpected bonus after losing.

Rumours have been doing the rounds about how prevalent serious, hardcore match-fixing is in non-league football for years. I can honestly say I've never personally been approached about throwing a match or taking a bribe to influence a result, but I think I'm seen as 'too clean' for anyone to bother with. However, I look at some of the refereeing decisions, some weird out-of-nowhere own goals and sloppy goalkeeping, and it just makes you wonder. Is it panic, incompetence – or is something else at play?

On internet betting, you can now put money on pretty much anything that happens during a match. What time will the first free kick be awarded? In what minute will the first corner be? So now we're told we have 'spot-fixing' where 'bent' players are paid to make sure these events happen at any given time. Spot-fixing is more difficult to detect than match-fixing, and its advantage is that one, lone player can carry out what needs doing without having to collude with anyone else on the pitch. Has it happened in matches I've played? It's so difficult to tell, although every now and again you watch a team-mate, under no pressure at all, put a ball out for a throw-in in the first few minutes and you get to wondering.

In truth, the non-league game is the ideal landscape for match-fixing as opposed to the big matches. When Premier League players are on £100,000 a week, I often think that even if they're remotely tempted, can you imagine the fortune you'd need to pay them off? Top-flight matches are all live on TV, filmed from multiple camera angles, moves and moments meticulously analysed by experts. If there was anything remotely untoward, it would be spotted immediately. Non-league is another matter altogether.

The lower down the pyramid you go, the more off the radar it becomes. With little TV coverage, glaring errors and dodgy-looking mistakes can't be instantly replayed. Once done, they're gone forever, off the record. There are, I'd imagine, vulnerable players to be had. Those in debt, those embittered by their club, their career, their situation. Those who are naturally bent and wouldn't need their arms twisted too hard. In a tiny minority no doubt, but when you're being paid a miniscule fraction of what the top players receive, the temptation could be overwhelming.

The globalised betting market has opened up the possibility of gambling anywhere and at any level, which makes detecting match-fixing even more difficult. Peruse our nation's biggest online betting sites and you'll soon find it's possible to place bets on everything from the Russian Premier Reserve Teams League to matches in the regional Norway Division 3 Group Five League. You can even put money on the Norwegian Junior Under-19s League. Conversely, out in the Far East, you can place bets on our National League, the Northern Premier, the Southern League, the Isthmian, the non-league list goes on, and a lot of people do so.

So, let me take you back to 2015, a year when the world of Asian betting was very much in the news. Thanks to an exhaustive investigation by the *Daily Telegraph*, police gathered enough evidence for the first time in decades to prosecute a group of match-fixers. Former Premier League player Delroy Facey and non-league footballer Moses Swaibu acted as the middlemen and were eventually jailed for their part in the plot. Both of them played for one of my former clubs at various points, but never when I was there.

Facey was found guilty of conspiracy to bribe non-league players, after approaching a footballer at struggling Hyde United. The Greater Manchester club had won promotion to the Conference Premier for the first time but were soon out of their depth. They managed to stay up in their first season, but the following campaign was an unmitigated disaster. They won only a single match and ended the season with just ten points – a record low.

Working with a Far East betting syndicate, Facey contacted a Hyde player, reminded him his team had been shit all season, so why not make some money out of it? Through Facey, the betting syndicate were prepared to pay the Hyde players £2,000 each if they contrived to concede four goals – two in each half – in a specific match. The Hyde player turned him down.

Two of the syndicate's ringleaders, 43-year-old Krishna Ganeshan and Singaporean national Chann Sankaran, were caught, tried and sentenced to five years each. Messages were found on their phones that implicated Facey, and he was sentenced to two and a half years behind bars. Moses Swaibu was found guilty of conspiracy to commit bribery and sentenced to six months in prison.

The club I was with at the time contained a few players who'd either played with or knew Facey and Swaibu. I remember me and my team-mates being shocked. We couldn't imagine how either of them could have been so dumb as to get involved in such dodgy business. But many of us were amazed at the sums of money involved. Most of us thought that £2,000 wasn't a figure you'd want to potentially risk ruining your career and your reputation over. You get caught and you're totally *persona non grata* in the world of football forever. However, the more skint among us could see how tempted they'd have been in the same situation. The more we talked and the more I thought about it, I began to understand. Even at our level, I was on much better pay than some of my team-mates, and we're talking hundreds not thousands here. And when you really think about it, non-league football in this country is the ideal place to bribe players.

A couple of years earlier, in 2013, something very strange was going on in National League South. It was on a night when the fixtures included Barcelona playing in a Champions League match and Welling matched up against Billericay Town. Chalk and cheese, you might say. Except that more money was staked on the Welling match through Asian betting exchanges than on the Spanish team's Champions League tie. Over £1m to be more precise. Billericay Town vehemently denied any wrongdoing and demanded that the FA investigate the situation. Nearly a decade on, we're all still waiting to hear what they found out.

So, you wonder, were these two isolated incidents, or the tip of an iceberg that suddenly became fleetingly visible? It's rumoured that various Far East crime syndicates and European mafia gangs are behind much of the illegal betting activity around the world, and that's no surprise. The global betting market for football is now worth a staggering $700bn annually.

If I was a footballer working for them, I'd most definitely keep my mouth shut on the matter and keep my head down. That may explain why we hear so little about it these days. If I was a corrupt player, I'd worry a lot more about my personal safety than being caught by the authorities, because I imagine that once a gang involves you in match-fixing, they come back with repeat demands. What if you say no?

If you can't trust that a football match is legitimate, as well as feeling cheated and conned, people will lose interest in the game.

Up for the Cup

THE FA Cup is still absolutely massive for non-league teams, and it really pisses me off that the top clubs don't seem to care much about it anymore. It takes the gloss off when they field the reserves and the kids. Back in the day, if Manchester United drew Chesterfield, they'd put out their best team. But not now. For me, it's the format of the Champions League and the Europa Cup that's done for it. Half the Premier League now regard it as the 'Consolation Cup', some silverware to be won if and when they get knocked out of Europe – the other half are fighting tooth and nail to stay in the Premier League so only seem to become interested in the later rounds. Like all of football, it is of course all about money – for non-league clubs too. A good cup run can sometimes mean the difference between a club managing to soldier on or folding completely, particularly further down the pyramid. A good run also gets a club in the spotlight and helps build its reputation, which helps when you're trying to attract good players.

In 2017, National League Lincoln City went on an astonishing run to the quarter-finals, eventually being beaten by Arsenal. It was the furthest a non-league team had gone in the FA Cup for over 100 years. Amazingly, in the previous round, the Gunners had knocked out tiny

Sutton United – the first time, along with Lincoln, that two non-league teams had made it to the fifth round for decades. There are those who'd argue that those lengthy FA Cup runs helped build the financial platform for first Lincoln, and then Sutton, to make it into League Two. Sutton earned over £700,000 from their cup journey – enough to cover their entire wage bill for the season. More recently, eighth-tier Marine AFC made it all the way to the FA Cup third round, eventually losing 5-0 to Tottenham Hotspur. That run, even without a crowd in the ground, made them £200,000 from TV rights, prize money and one-off sponsorships.

I've made it into the first round proper quite a few times with various clubs, but the second round is the furthest I've got. That proved to be a total anticlimax. We were all hoping to be drawn against a big League One team and ended up playing away to a fellow National League team. Never mind, we thought, beat them and we might get a plum draw against a Premier League team in the third round. We lost to a single goal, scored in the 90th minute.

What I love about it is that it's the luck of the draw, completely in the lap of the gods. And, in a way, the smaller clubs have a psychological advantage because they've nothing to lose. No one's expecting you to win, so it kind of frees up your mind, which can sometimes be a leveller. People underestimate psychology and mindset in football. When you're playing for the bigger team, you worry you might be in for a long day and then the nerves kick in. The smaller team, it's your day in the sun, so the adrenalin kicks in and pushes you.

That's how it was when the National League team I played for drew Huddersfield in a first round match. At the time, the Terriers were top of League One and they started the match with confidence and swagger. But thanks to some stout defending and the odd slice of luck, we went in at half-time still level. Same again in the second half and as the minutes ticked away you could sense that the Huddersfield players were growing ever more panicked. We made it over the line to draw 0-0 and went up to Yorkshire for the replay. This time, Town started the match jittery and fitful. Psychologically, I felt as if we'd got inside their heads. They were without doubt the better-quality players but seemed to be playing within themselves. In the end we lost, and you could feel the wave of relief amongst the Huddersfield players.

Before non-league teams get to the first round proper and join the EFL clubs, there's the small matter of qualifying, which is a long and winding road. The simple truth is, the further down the pyramid you are, the more qualifying rounds you have to play. For the 2021/22 FA Cup, the likes of White Ensign FC and Erith & Belvedere started their campaign way back in early August in the extra preliminary round. Following that was a preliminary round and then six further qualifying rounds. Eventually, 32 non-league clubs progress to the first round proper to join the 46 League One and Two clubs.

The prize money is a real bonus for players at the non-league level. The most I've been paid for getting through a round has been £500. If you're on the telly, that's even more money. The players from Lincoln and Sutton will have had good summer holidays that year. However, at a couple of my clubs, the directors did a real dirty on us. At both, they promised us that as well as any prize money we won in the cup competitions, they'd pay us a percentage of the gates too. At both clubs we enjoyed long runs in the FA Cup and the FA Trophy. After we eventually went out, the players asked for their bonuses and, on both occasions, the directors pleaded poverty and refused to stump up the money. I'm still waiting.

The FA Cup isn't the only knockout trophy dear to non-league hearts. For the bigger outfits there's the FA Trophy – or to give the competition its full title, the Football Association Challenge Trophy. This is open to clubs playing at Tiers 5–8 of the overall football pyramid, which covers the National League Premier, National Leagues North and South, the Southern League, Isthmian League and Northern Premier. Then there's the FA Vase, or Football Association Challenge Vase, which is basically for all the non-league clubs in the tiers below that, which is well over 600 teams. With that many sides competing, it has two preliminary rounds, six rounds proper, a two-leg semi-final and then a Wembley final. The winning club takes home £30,000 prize money and a share of the Wembley gate, which is truly life-sustaining for a small club.

Both of these cups represent an opportunity that few Football League players will ever get near – playing a final at Wembley. For example, during the past ten years the likes of Everton, Newcastle, Wolves, Brighton, Burnley and Leeds United haven't appeared in a final at Wembley, never mind many of the clubs in the current Championship. But thanks to the FA Vase, Northern Premier League Division One side Warrington Rylands and Isthmian League South Central Division Binfield have. So too have Hebburn Town from the Northern Premier League Division One East, and tiny Cray Valley Paper Mills FC, whose Isthmian League South East Division ground holds less than a thousand.

I've been there twice as a player in FA Trophy finals – once as a starter, the second time as a sub. The former represents my greatest day in football – and that, bearing in mind we lost. I was in my early twenties but felt like a kid in a sweet shop. There were 60,000 people in the stadium and the match was shown live on Sky Sports. The biggest crowd I'd ever played in front of before this was 14,000.

We stayed for three days in a really swish hotel and prepared for the big day at the FA's old training base at Bisham Abbey. The night before, I couldn't sleep a wink, which I discovered the following morning was a fate shared by most of my team-mates.

The following day our luxury coach swept us across London and dropped us at the players' entrance. As I gazed up at Wembley's high walls, it all started to feel very real and my legs turned to jelly. Walking through the stadium halls and corridors your eyes are drawn to the framed photos of Bobby Moore lifting the World Cup, Bobby Charlton in action, Gazza beating a man, Lineker whipping in a goal. And, as you look, you realise you're standing on the shoulders of giants in this, the home of football.

We walked into what was to be our dressing room for the day, and I felt utterly overwhelmed. It must have been ten times the size of my club's home dressing room. The treatment room looked like a high-tech hospital ward, and there was even a warm-up area complete with artificial turf. We got changed and started a little banter, but you could tell that everyone was just desperate to get out there and start the match. As a non-league player this is as big time as it gets and the effect that the palatial surroundings of Wembley have upon you is immense.

It was goosebumps time when we ran out. Bear in mind, I was more used to playing at non-league grounds and I'd never been on a pitch quite like that. It looked and felt as though an army of ground staff had cut the grass with manicure scissors. I gazed up into those gigantic stands and spotted my dad, my uncle and a bunch of old school friends, and felt a sharp surge of pride. I looked around the ground at bank after bank of fans. The noise was deafening, and I remember thinking, *Is this really me? Am I really doing this?* All those early knockbacks in my career, all of it was worth it for this.

For the first few minutes I was incredibly nervous. But I had a few good touches early on and that gave me a confidence boost. The pitch looked massive and I've never experienced noise like it, before or since. It was so incessantly loud that our manager couldn't get any orders or information to us. I was out on the wing and nearest to him, but still couldn't pick up a word. No matter, we scored first, and six or seven of us slid on our knees together towards the corner flag. Think about how ecstatic you'd be if your team scored at Wembley. Times that by ten and that's how you feel as a player. In that moment, I'd never been happier. But football, of course, is all about ups and downs. We got pegged back and eventually lost the match 2-1. So it was a loser's medal for me. Even so, I wouldn't swap that day for anything.

My return visit a few years later was decidedly anticlimactic. It was exciting to be back at Wembley, but I was back in very different circumstances. The club I was with for that final had been an unhappy move for me all season. I'd been a bench-warmer for months before the Wembley appearance and had been pretty much frozen out by the manager. I was actually surprised to be named on the bench, rather than left to sit in the stands, but being there for a second time was a hollow experience. Of course, I wanted us to win, but my time at the club had been a vexing and frustrating one where I'd never felt as if I belonged. I'd become an outsider there and even being at Wembley again didn't much lift my spirits. The day proved to be decidedly low-key. We were second-best throughout the match. I got to come on with ten minutes to go when we were losing and had little time to offer any meaningful contribution to the cause. We conceded another goal in injury time, which all felt yawningly inevitable.

There's one other cup competition that a small select band of National League clubs have taken part in over the last few years – somewhat bizarrely, the Scottish Professional Football League Challenge Cup. When I first heard about this from a mate who plays at Sutton United, I thought it was either an April Fool's or a wind-up. But it's absolutely true. From the 2016/17 season onwards, the Scottish Challenge Cup's organisers came up with a strange idea. As well as featuring all Scottish professional and semi-pro teams, they rather strangely decided to invite selected teams from the National League and part-time clubs from Wales, Northern Ireland and the Republic of Ireland to take part. Answers on a postcard please!

Sutton and Boreham Wood fleetingly took part, with Sutton enjoying an 800-mile round trip to play Airdrieonians along the way. In 2018/19, Connah's Quay Nomads from the Cymru Premier beat Edinburgh City 5-4 in the cup's semi-final, and became the first non-Scottish team to contest the Scottish Professional Football League Challenge Cup Final, although they were neither professional nor Scottish. It's a funny old game is football! Scotland prevailed on the day, with Ross County beating the Welsh team 3-1 at Caley Thistle's Caledonian Stadium up there in Inverness. Last I heard, the pandemic had put paid to non-Scottish involvement in the competition, and thus the National League's brief foray on to Scottish soil.

Some of my favourite matches have been in the cup competitions. I love that knockout element, where it's all about who manages to lift themselves most on the day. Often it can be a welcome distraction from the dull trudge of a mediocre season, particularly if your team has been on a bad run, not played well and is down in the dumps confidence-wise. It's a one-off match where everything seems possible. A chance to renew hope and optimism within the team and allow a player the opportunity to dream. Because at the end of the day, most footballers are dreamers. To even think you could make a living out of the game is a crazy thought. Cup matches are good for the soul, so I'm always up for the cup.

The Non-League Lions

THE FA Cup, the Trophy and the Vase all give non-league players a rare chance to have their moment in the sun. But beyond gaining medals as cup winners or league champions, perhaps the greatest honour for any footballer is to pull on the shirt of their country. To represent your nation is the ultimate accolade, but surely not one open to non-league footballers. Think again.

Outside of non-league football, it's a little-known fact that England has a team made up of players from outside the Premier League and the EFL. So, let me welcome you to the almost secret world of England C. I'll be surprised if many general football fans have even heard of them, which is why I want to use this book as an opportunity to give England's 'unknown' national team some coverage. Because I owe them one. In my early twenties, England C came a-calling, and I turned them down.

I know, I know. Who throws away the chance of playing for England? Your honour, in my defence there were mitigating circumstances. It was at the end of a long, exhausting season. My club had gone a long way in all the cup competitions, I was an ever-present in the team throughout the entire league programme and by the end of the campaign I'd played well over 50 full matches. For the last few I was running on empty, utterly fatigued, physically and mentally.

Having suffered from burnout before and wrecking half a season for myself, I took the tough decision to turn down the chance of playing for England C. I spoke with my manager and explained the situation and he agreed it was the wisest thing to do. He didn't want me coming back for pre-season already exhausted. My dad, however, thought I was a lunatic. 'What if,' he asked, 'you turn them down and they never come back to pick you?' I reassured him that I'd speak personally to the England C management team and explain the circumstances. I was sure they'd understand. After all, it wasn't just a one-off match. They had a couple of matches and a two-week camp. I did speak to the management team and they didn't understand. In fact, they were furious. How dare I turn down such an honour? They clearly thought I was some kind of diva. My copybook was well and truly blotted.

Instead, I went away on what turned out to be a supremely relaxing fortnight's holiday in Spain with a couple of team-mates. It was the break I desperately needed. But when I told my team-mates about the whole thing, they agreed with my dad. I was a lunatic. Not surprisingly, I was never approached by England C again. Now, in hindsight, I hugely regret my decision. More than a few time, I've visualised pulling on that England shirt and it never gets easier, knowing I blew it.

Now in my thirties I'm well over their age limit. To play for England C you have to be a non-league player, 23 years old or under. To understand why this should be the case, we need to look at some history. Prior to 1974, England had a very well-established amateur national team and a very successful one at that. Formed in 1901, its first match was a 12-0 win over Germany at White Hart Lane. In 1906, they beat the France amateur team 15-0 and from 1906–1910, were unbeaten in 20 matches. England's players effectively made up the Great Britain football teams that won Olympic gold medals at the London Games in 1908 and at Stockholm in 1912. Throughout the following six decades, the England team mainly played against other major European nations, and from 1953/54 until 1973/74, competed for the British Amateur Championship with Scotland, Wales and Northern Ireland – a competition they won on 16 occasions. Then in 1974, amateur football became no more.

With the rise of semi-professionalism in non-league, the FA decided it was time to put an end to the distinction between amateur and professional football, which sadly meant the end of the England amateur team. But it can't have been a good look for the home of football not to be represented internationally in the world of non-league football, so in 1979 the England Non-League team was established. Their first manager was future England national team boss Howard Wilkinson, and between 1979 and 2008, they took part each year in the Four Nations Tournament alongside non-league Scotland and Wales representatives and the full international Gibraltar team, winning it seven times. Along the way they had a name change to England C, and from 2003 were helmed by former Hertford Town, Stevenage and Barnet manager Paul Fairclough. They also played friendly matches against the likes of the Italy C and the Netherlands non-league teams.

As time went by, it became harder for England C to not only find opponents of a comparable skill level, but countries who could afford to fund decent international non-league teams on a regular basis. So, the decision was made to spread the net wider and England C approached international under-23 teams, who were looking for opponents as warm-up matches for their European Cup tournaments. To make it a more level playing field, England C agreed to only field players aged 23 or under. Since then, they've played full under-23 international sides from the likes of Russia, Belgium, Turkey, Latvia, Estonia and Slovakia, plus further friendlies against the Czech Republic and Cyprus under-21s, Ukraine under-20s and Hungary's under-19s. It's testament to England C's high levels of performance that they've never been embarrassed in any of these matches against young international footballers, many of whom play for top European clubs. Their biggest loss was in 2017, a 4-0 defeat to Slovakia under-23s, but bear in mind that the Slovakian team contained players who turned out for Benfica, Sampdoria and Lille.

On average, the team get to play four or five times a year, usually in the international windows and close season. The number of matches they can play is also limited by their small budget, and most players only get to play a handful of matches. But players are presented with a proper international cap for each match and get to wear, and keep, a Three Lions England shirt that has the letter 'C' embroidered underneath the badge. It still eats away at me that they could be sitting in my living room cabinet right now.

To add insult to injury, when I've talked to other players about what the set-up is like with England C, they all speak very highly of the manager Paul Fairclough and his team. Things are clearly tight money-wise and the players don't get much time together. Usually when they have a Tuesday night match, they meet up on the Sunday, train on the Monday and then play the following day. With so few hours in one another's company, Fairclough concentrates a lot on team-bonding. And because many of the England C matches are basically friendlies and they're not locked into the weekly grind of win at all costs, he encourages his players to express themselves. That can be a liberating change for footballers who are drilled to get three points, and players always say he makes the England C experience a lot of fun.

Fairclough's a man who has a long background in non-league so really understands the players and goes out of his way to ensure the best performers are being noticed and selected, whether that be in the National leagues or below. There's a scouting team of ten, all of whom cover a specific geographical area and watch clubs at all levels of the non-league football pyramid. To make sure more people get to hear about the England C team, Fairclough tries to have matches played across the north, south and Midlands. Over the last few years, they've played everywhere from Salford City to Solihull Moors and Leyton Orient. Perhaps the most amazing thing about Paul Fairclough is that he's been doing this job for nearly 20 years, which makes him England national football's longest-serving manager ever. Now into his early seventies, he's still going strong.

Often the England C set-up becomes a victim of its own success. After each successive transfer window passes, the team loses more regulars to EFL clubs and yet another rebuild has to begin. Fairclough estimates that around 200 players who've turned out for England C have since gone on to join Premier League and EFL clubs, although he's always keen to point out that it's the individuals and their clubs that have done all the hard work towards that. But the truth is that appearing for England C has offered them the rare opportunity to be in the shop window as dozens of scouts and agents turn up for all their matches. What better place to have a close look at the very best of non-league football's young talent all in one place? In fact, it's the only place.

An extraordinary pool of players have made that leap. Craig Mackail-Smith spent his early career at St Albans City and Dagenham & Redbridge, and played seven times for England C, scoring four goals. He then moved into EFL football with Peterborough, Brighton and Luton, scoring over 100 goals along the way and winning seven international caps with Scotland. Andre Gray earned six caps for England C while playing for Luton Town, then moved on to Brentford, Burnley, Watford and QPR. Pacy defender Andy Yiadom has enjoyed an amazing career since winning his four England C caps, leaving Braintree to play for Barnet in League Two and then moving into the Championship with Barnsley and Reading. As well as notching up over 150 matches in England's second tier, Andy has won 14 caps for the full Ghana national team, because although born in England, his parents are Ghanaian. Forward Fejiri Okenabirhie won five caps and scored four times for the C team. He started off at Stevenage and Harrow Borough, before moving into League One.

Other players who've turned out for England C include former Hinckley United and Solihull Moors striker Omar Bogle, who's now playing for Doncaster Rovers in League One; former Halifax defender Matty Pearson, who went on to play over 100 times for Luton Town in League One and the Championship and is now at Huddersfield Town; and striker James Norwood, who started his career with Eastbourne Town and is now at Ipswich Town in League One. Norwood scored a hat-trick for England C in what's still their record score of 6-1, against the full Bermuda national team.

An important new dimension to England C's work has been in helping to support the football development of emerging nations and communities – and of displaced refugees. In 2013, the squad spent a week in Bermuda, playing the national team and doing outreach coaching and training work with children around Bermuda's schools. The players became celebrities on the island and the match against Bermuda was shown live on TV. The 6-1 winning team included two future Premier League players in Andre Gray and Sam Clucas. In 2017, England C played the Punjab national team at the Solihull Moors Damson Park. This is a team that represents the Punjabi community across the world and, for this match, all the Punjab players were drawn from the English non-league.

During their time in Jordan in 2014 preparing for their match against that country's under-23s, the squad played a mini tournament with young football-mad Syrian refugees. Most non-league footballers never get the chance to play outside of Britain, and England C offers the opportunity to broaden horizons and learn a little more about other cultures – and how important football is around the world.

Paul Fairclough is also in charge of organising special representative teams for the FA, most of which he puts together from players in the lower leagues of the football pyramid. In 2018, Fairclough took a young 16-strong FA Representative XI squad 16,000 miles down to the Falkland Islands on a goodwill visit. His players included Ibrahim Olutade, who plays for Hanwell Town, and Alex Paine of Chalfont St Peter. Both clubs play down in the Isthmian League South Central Division. Jonathan Lacey was a Leverstock Green player, who are part of the Spartan South Midlands League. Liam Ferdinand turned out for Bracknell Town in the Isthmian League South Central Division. Captain Mitchell Parker played for Reading City.

With an average age of just 21, the young players and their staff spent several days in the island's three schools coaching children and staff. They also played two matches on the island – a 3-1 win against the Falkland Islands team, who regularly play in the Island Games, a biannual multi-sports event for island communities around the world; and a second against a British Forces South Atlantic Islands side, a 3-2 win for the FA Representative XI. Both matches drew the largest-ever crowds for football on the Falkland Islands. The squad were there for Remembrance Day and laid a wreath from the FA at the Port Stanley war memorial. The trip must have been a life-changing experience for this squad of young non-league players. This is what we need more of in our sport.

Similar to the rest of the non-league football world, the pandemic has affected England C hugely. They had two friendly matches cancelled in 2020; one against Wales C, and a second against the Nepal full international team, which was to be another important step forward in England C's attempts to bind the wider football community together. It was deliberately scheduled to be played in Aldershot – a town that contains Britain's largest Nepalese community. Let's hope that it can be rescheduled. As a consequence, England C have been in limbo and not played a match since losing 2-0 to the Estonia's under-23 team in June 2019 – a match, incidentally, where Estonia fielded six full internationals. I hope they can get out there playing again soon and kick-start their momentum.

One thing I find heartbreaking for the England C team is that, although they're officially a member of the 'FA family', they've never played at Wembley. As all their home matches have taken place at lower EFL and non-league grounds, wouldn't it be fitting if, when they do re-emerge, one of their next matches could see the FA celebrate their own England C and all their work by organising a fixture for them at our national stadium? Perhaps a match before an under-21s match or, god forbid, prior to a full international friendly maybe. It seems such a shame that the FA hasn't given them more visibility, but in many ways it seems to me that it reflects the story of the FA's relationship with non-league football. In every sense of the words, we're always the poor relations. Now more than ever we need the FA to give proactive, strong and meaningful support to non-league football, because Covid has hit it hard.

The St Pauli of non-league football – Dulwich Hamlet and their Ultras.

The world's oldest football grandstand at Great Yarmouth FC's Wellesley Recreation Ground.

The toughest of opponents, midfield maestro Emmanuel Panther.

Build it and they will come – FC United of Manchester's Broadhurst Stadium.

Dartford FC's eco-friendly new Princes Park ground.

Revolutionary chairman Dale Vince watches his Forest Green Rovers v Grimsby.

AFC Fylde's Danny Rowe with the FA Trophy in 2019.

From non-league to the Championship – inspirational manager Danny Cowley.

The other national football team – England C players before their 2018 match against Wales C.

Warrington Rylands celebrate winning the 2020/21 FA Vase.

Much travelled nomad Jefferson Louis in action for Rushden & Diamonds v Wrexham.

One of my favourite managers, Gary Mills.

Covid

THEN THE world changed. My first brush with Covid was on a Tuesday night in Stafford. It was an away match on a rainy winter's evening, and as we left our cars and piled into the dressing room, it soon became clear that one of our team-mates wasn't well at all. His face was grey, and the sweating, wheezing and coughing made it clear to all and sundry he'd not be taking to the pitch that night. At first, we thought he had a touch of the flu, but then one of the coaching staff asked him whether he could smell anything. He couldn't, and suddenly the penny began to drop. It was still early days and, although of course we'd all heard of Covid, none of us were really sure what it involved – apart from losing your sense of smell.

Sure enough, our sick team-mate took a test the next day and it came up positive. One or two other players followed suit and shortly after that our next league match was called off because of Covid infections within the club. Everyone was put into isolation. At that point there had been the first small tragic wave of deaths, which seemed to mainly be amongst elderly people who had pre-existing health problems. We were all fit young men and surely had little to worry about aside from a really nasty bout of mega-flu.

We got back on to the training pitch a couple of weeks later, but now everything was different. There had been an escalation in the number of deaths, and by no means were all of them the old or infirm. A few people at the club had family or friends or neighbours who'd died. We were being tested every day we came into training, had to wear face masks in the dressing room and train as much as possible at a social distance, with regular handwash stops. As the death rates began to soar nationally, there was a strange, sober feeling around the club. We all began to realise that this was something really serious. The squad developed a slightly nervy Dunkirk spirit. As soon as a player returned from Covid, everyone would interrogate them to make sure all their symptoms had gone. Otherwise, we continued to do what we do – we trained and played football matches. For a while.

As more players and their families up and down the country caught Covid, an increasing number of matches began to be called off every week. With the R-rate forever rising and a dizzying backlog of cancelled matches beginning to pile up, the powers that be had little choice but to close the season prematurely. The players all hated it. To not finish a season was unthinkable. I remembered reading about how football seasons were prematurely wound up during the two world wars and thinking at the time how cheated the players must have felt. Now I knew.

Everyone was left in limbo land. Those of us with contracts were furloughed and at least managed to get 80 per cent of our pay every month. Those without weren't so lucky and a few of my team-mates had to apply for Universal Credit to get by. Even those of us on furlough were struggling. According to sportingintelligence.com's last annual survey into global sports salaries, Premier League players earn an average of £3m a year. At National League level, most players – me included – play from pay cheque to pay cheque. When that's cut by 20 per cent, on the level of wages we're on, some bills have to wait.

But at least I still had a club. As the weeks and months passed and summer approached, I got more and more texts and calls from players I knew at other clubs who'd been released. Many of them were, like me, older players who were amongst the top earners at their respective clubs, including one of my former teams, who had no choice but to have a clear-out and replace their experienced players with younger kids who didn't cost much. Suddenly I seemed to know dozens of players in their late twenties and early thirties who were desperate for a club, any club. Some of them prematurely decided to call it a day.

Because non-league clubs are such an important part of their communities, a lot of them stepped up during Covid to help their local elderly, the isolated and the financially hard up. Some set up food banks and delivered food parcels. Others laid on helplines. Hampton & Richmond Borough supported the most vulnerable by organising a shopping and medical prescription collection service. Maidenhead United launched a community care programme, which even included a dog-walking service for those locals who were self-isolating. Stockport County raised over £75,000 for their local NHS.

As soon as lockdown began, my club proved to be very tech savvy. We had regular Zoom calls from the fitness coaches, who put us through our paces for an hour and helped keep our morale up, mental health-wise. I, for one, found the lockdown to be very isolating. I had my partner in the house with me, but I struggled without the rhythm and routine of going into training regularly with my team-mates and, of course, playing matches. It was like being out with a long-term injury, only you couldn't go anywhere to lift your spirits or relieve the boredom.

As players, we set up a WhatsApp group and regularly talked, shared experiences and generally tried to have a laugh. That definitely helped, as did individual Zoom calls from the manager, who regularly rang us all to chat through any concerns we might be having – physical, mental or, in some cases, financial. I did everything I could to stay fit, but of course all the gyms were closed. The coaching team gave us individualised fitness programmes to do at home, but it's joyless training on your own. It was a pleasure to get out into the fresh air and go on long runs, but again that got to become a lonely experience. My partner and I hit the delivery takeaway scene big time. For the first time in my career, I was putting on weight, which I didn't like one bit. It was only half a stone, but I've a slight build and an extra three or four kilos soon shows up. I felt sluggish and unfit, which was an alien feeling for me during a summer break, let alone during an actual season.

As the months dragged by, I began to realise that life was becoming tougher for the club. They'd been given a few small government grants and the furlough money, but that was it. All three income streams they so relied upon had now been cut off – no ticket sales from matches, no revenue from the clubhouse and, as most local firms were struggling themselves, very little in the way of sponsorship money. This was reflected around the world of non-league, where hospitality and club bars closed overnight. Community activities and facility hire – often a gold mine for clubs – all stopped, and the income tap was well and truly switched off. In the season they achieved promotion into League Two, Sutton reckon the lockdown cost them £200,000 in lost revenue. In context, their entire playing budget for that season was £300,000.

It cost Altrincham a packet just to play in the National North play-offs. The three behind-closed-doors matches left them with a bill of £50,000 because they had to take their players off furlough and pay for extensive Covid testing. Typical non-league – the Altrincham fans raised £45,000 towards paying the bill.

The ever-amazing army of volunteers at my club continued to do maintenance around the ground, kept the pitch in good condition and generally did all they could to keep the club ticking over. But there was an air of quiet desperation the further into the pandemic we went. Our volunteers were in constant turmoil, trying to respond to each new confusing set of Covid guidelines they were given, which seemed to change almost day by day. They were the ones who not only had to put the precautions in place and police them but had to do so with far less resources than bigger clubs.

Showing their usual doggedness, volunteers around the country ingeniously thought up new ways to make some money just to keep their outfits afloat. Fans at my club ran online quizzes and raffles. Hampton & Richmond Borough raised £10,000 raffling off the naming rights to their stadium. A couple of my former clubs signed up with crowdfunding sites and another set up its first-ever online shop from scratch. Thanks to the amazing fundraising efforts of their fans, Chester FC were handed over £115,000 via the supporters' 'Boost the Budget' campaign, to help keep them alive. In a bid to create a new regular income stream, eighth-tier Daventry Town of the Southern League Division One Central paid a company to lay on big-screen drive-in movie nights at their ground.

Fortunately, with the help of our loyal fans, my club managed to financially squeak its way through the lockdowns and the match cancellations. Other clubs weren't so lucky. Staff lost their jobs; some went out of business. One of the UK's oldest clubs, Rhyl, had to be wound up, with directors blaming the financial impact of Covid. That was 141 years of history gone down the Swanee – a club who'd won the Welsh Cup four times and were former Welsh champions. The Rhyl who'd given us players like Barry Horne and Lee Trundle. Football fans in Rhyl have been fundraising and trying to form a new club, but at the very best it's back to square one down at the bottom of their football pyramid, if they can make it work. Droylsden FC, who've been around since 1892, resigned from the Northern Premier because of the financial toll the pandemic has had on the club.

I'm surprised that more non-league clubs didn't go under, but perhaps that final reckoning is yet to come. Those that survive will have slimmed-down squads on generally smaller wages, which will see a lot of good, skilful players finding it impossible to find a club at the level they're used to playing. Cost-cutting will be the order of the day because unless you have a rich owner it's a hand-to-mouth existence for most clubs even during the best of times.

Even for those with a wealthy owner, what happens if they decide to pull out? This has been an ongoing question in non-league football, which Covid highlighted big time. What's better? One person putting a lot in or many putting a little in? Do you want your club's ambition to be fighting for promotions or fighting to become sustainable, so that whatever your league position, you're still in business in ten years' time?

I know what most players would say – we want promotions and success. It's only natural. As a sportsman you want to win. But looking at the bigger picture, could the future of non-league football now be forced to edge more towards fan-owned clubs? In the long term, they look a much more sustainable route than the private model because, let's face it, if the latter, you're only ever one sale away from a bad owner.

FC United of Manchester have made a lot of people in football think differently about fan-owned clubs. In National League North they regularly pull 2,000-plus fans to each home match, into a ground that the supporters planned, funded and built. As a player in non-league, for me it's been one of the most enjoyable places to play. The fans are committed and passionate, the matchday atmosphere there electric, but friendly and welcoming. As you go down the pyramid, more clubs have become fan-owned. Worcester City for example, are now a really well-run outfit, with the many contributing.

Perhaps the only downside to fan-owned clubs is to do with why supporters have had to take that route. To wit, someone else has screwed up their club and the only way forward out of an often dire situation is for the fans to take over. That frequently means their most urgent job is to clear up the financial mess the previous owners have left them in. And that takes a lot of work and commitment. Fortunately, my experience of non-league fans is that they'll sacrifice anything to keep their club running. And they think well out of the box. That's never been more evident than in the way many clubs have tried to navigate a way through the pandemic.

One thing is for sure, those clubs without a millionaire owner will struggle in the next few years. The new order of the day will be more about survival off the pitch than success on it. Any club that bets the house on trying to get promotion will need their collective heads examining. They'll also have to deal with unexpected consequences of the pandemic that have taken a longer time to understand. Medical staff and physios are experts in rehabbing players through fractures, pulls and strains – but how do you treat the effects of Long Covid? We already have two players at my club who are in and out with their health and fitness, suffering from symptoms such as muscle pain, feelings of exhaustion and lung trouble. What's the best way to help them? And in an already slimmed-down squad, how will the manager cope with two players, and possibly more in the future, who are suffering from Long Covid?

The relief of getting back out on to the pitch to actually play competitive matches again was massive. And although we were only allowed 30 per cent of our usual crowd size back for the early matches, it was glorious to hear chanting and cheering and to see supporters enjoying themselves in the ground. There were numerous times during the height of the pandemic when I seriously worried whether we'd ever get back to that kind of normality again.

Part-Timers

CALLING SOMEONE a part-timer is sometimes a derogatory term for someone who's seen to be not pulling their weight. That couldn't be less true than in non-league football. As I've recently become a proper part-time player for the first time in my footballing life, trying to juggle playing with a full-time teaching career, I'm finding out first-hand what bloody hard work it is. Previously, as a full-time professional, I'd witnessed it all from a distance. Teammates moaning about their bosses, who were complaining about them taking more time off to travel to matches or coming in for training when they were down to do some overtime or a different shift. Or not, and the coaching staff getting annoyed at their no-show and invariably marking them down for the bench come Saturday. Now I know what it feels like to be forever serving two masters. It's a bloody pressure and I'm learning how much self-discipline and energy you need to keep standards high in both your daytime job and in your football career.

Teaching these days is a job and a half and it came as a shock to me. I had no idea how many countless hours I'd have to spend in the evenings and at weekends on preparation, marking, organising and running extra-curricular activities; speaking to students and parents and carers; writing match reports for the school website; as well as actually teaching five full-on days a week, in at school from 7am most mornings. But the real pressure comes from the individual pupils. I teach PE and Sport in an inner-city secondary school that's in special measures and every single one of my classes seems to have a hardcore of genuine troublemakers whose behaviour is often appalling. Just trying to keep order in those lessons is an achievement in itself. It's the kind of stress I've never experienced before, and it's exhausting. I used to hear about these things from friends who are teachers and, although I never thought they were over-exaggerating, I'd think, well, that's what you do, it's part of the job. Now I get it.

While I'm teaching full-time and on a new part-time contract at my club, I have two bosses who both believe they have first call on me, and why shouldn't they? Recently, the school organised a week of parents' evenings, which was a big problem for me. The Tuesday night session clashed with a regional cup match. At the same time I was meant to be kicking off the match, I was also scheduled to be across a desk from Joe Bloggs and his mum and dad, discussing his progress in maths. On this occasion, the manager was really understanding and told me that, as it was only a minor cup match, he was thinking of giving me a rest anyway. This time it worked out. But what will happen when a parents' evening or some other important school function clashes with an important league match? That hasn't cropped up yet, but it will, and I'm not sure what I'll do for the best. As club captain I feel a real responsibility to set a good example. We've had players cry off matches in the past because of work commitments and I must admit I've always been the first to be disappointed and urge them to get their act together. Now I'm in the same boat and have a far keener understanding of the problems part-time players face.

One positive thing that teaching has brought me is a new definite routine, which has been welcome. Talking to players who've retired, one of the things they've found the hardest is losing the routine of being a footballer. Your life is mapped out from pre-season through to the final day of each campaign. You know when you'll be training, when the matches are and that all the arrangements to make them happen will be done for you. There's a comfort to that. Similarly, being a teacher, someone else sorts out the curriculum, you're told where to turn up and when, and you pretty much know what the score is for your coming 'campaign'. That's been good, because I know that many full-time footballers who've found it really difficult to transition into retirement and working in new jobs have felt lost and depressed.

The problem I'm currently trying to resolve is learning to fit in everything else. I train two full evenings every week and often I'll be scrambling into my car following an after-school match without going home or eating. I turn up at the ground, quickly change into my kit and go straight out to training. I play a match every Saturday, and in midweek a dozen or so times every season. Then I need to have some kind of life beyond that with my partner and family and friends. I've never juggled so many balls in the air at one time. A lot of people struggle to get a work-life balance with just one job, but this is hard work. How players who also have young families manage it, I just don't know.

Throughout my entire career, this is the least I've trained outside of club training sessions. I used to visit the gym two or three times a week and have at least a couple of long runs. These days, zero, nothing. Psychologically,

I HOPE YOU DIE OF CANCER

I come home from school so totally worn out that I don't have the motivation to do much more than hit the sofa. Currently, I feel guilty and unfit. When I used to play full-time, I'd be in for training four or five days every week. Now, as a part-timer, it's two sessions a week, which means the coaching staff have to be far more focused and quickly push us through what we need to do for the match ahead.

There's not a lot of fitness work in the sessions, more working out tactical play and how we can hurt the opposition. We'll do 11 vs 11s to practise set plays and how our team is to be set up. We go through the other team's strengths and weaknesses, but not in as much detail. As a full-time pro, we'd have the luxury of time out on the training pitch doing a lot more actual practical work on how to nullify or exploit certain individual opponents. Part-time clubs simply don't have the time for that level of in-depth work. It's amazing what the coaching staff can fit into those two evenings though, and they're pretty full-on. I'm well knackered by the time I get home.

When I think back to all those years of being full-time, I realise how easy I had it. You'd go into the club for training, and breakfast was laid on for you. There would be two or three hours of training and then you were fed lunch. In the car, drive home and the rest of the day is yours. The difference between being full-time and part-time in non-league football is massive and I'm still struggling to adjust.

I already feel the difference in more subtle ways too. Only meeting up twice a week for training means there's not quite the same bond or understanding between the players. When you're kicking a football around together, day in and day out, you learn a lot about the abilities of the team-mates around you and how they like to play. You know how they move and where they find space, so you can start to anticipate their runs. That training time together is particularly important when new players are introduced into the squad and you're all trying to learn one another's game. It's a frustration for me that I can no longer do this, because I've spent most of my career preparing well. This is the reality of part-time football.

Here's another reality. Naturally as a footballer you want to play at as high a level as you can. But the promise of opportunities can present big dilemmas for ambitious part-time players. Imagine you lived in the north and a League Two club in the Midlands or the south came in and wanted to sign you full-time. A professional footballer at last. All you ever dreamed of. Happy days! Or maybe not.

Harsh economic realities instantly come into play. So, imagine this, the contract you're offered is for about the same money you're earning in your current full-time job, which obviously you'd have to quit. But you'll be doing a lot of extra travelling because your professional club is over 100 miles away, which will effectively make you worse off. Plus, it's only a one-year contract, which means you'll be giving up a stable job for something a lot more precarious. And you have a young family who are depending on you to bring home the bacon. So, what are you going to do? I know quite a few players who've found themselves in this situation and I've really felt for them.

What I now earn from my full-time teaching job dwarfs what I earn as a part-time footballer. Would I give it up if a higher league club came in with a half-decent offer? Probably not because it wouldn't come near to what I earn as a teacher. Into my late twenties and early thirties, I'd have jumped, for example, at an offer to play back in League Two, and I honestly think I'd have been good enough to do so.

Now I'm in my mid-thirties and near to playing retirement, the reality of what's ahead of me is setting in.

Is there 'the perfect job' to fit in alongside being a part-time player? In my naivety, I used to think it might be sports teacher, because it helps keep you fit and connected every day in thinking about tactics and organising people. Then I became a teacher! Now I think it's probably the self-employed who have a bit more flexibility in terms of organising their own work time and can fit in around club commitments a little easier.

The different jobs that players have outside the game is mind-boggling. I've played alongside undertakers, policemen, IT consultants, accountants and financial advisors – even a guy who worked as a psychologist in a mental prison. At one time or another, no matter how sympathetic their employers, all of them have had problems fitting their jobs around playing part-time football. One of my current team-mates is a role model to us all though, in terms of being supremely well organised. He's a medical rep manager and is so good at time management that he leads Zoom meetings with his staff and clients on the coach to matches and in the dressing room beforehand. I've had a team-mate who worked night shifts as a supermarket shelf stacker, and he'd often come in for matches on a couple of hours' sleep, still seemingly full of beans.

Part of it depends on your mindset and how good you are at organising your time. For some part-timers, it's much more to do with physical tiredness and powers of recovery. The players who make my mind boggle the most are the guys who work in hard manual labour – construction work, refuse work and the like. They work demanding physical jobs all day and then train and play football. One of my current team-mates is a gardener and, for most months of the year, he's out from sun-up to sundown digging, weeding, lifting, pushing and pulling – and yet skips into training sessions with the energy of a Duracell bunny.

There are a few part-time players who manage to successfully co-exist in what appear to be two totally mutually exclusive worlds. Maidenhead's French defender Remy Clerima is a model pro in every sense of the words. When he's not turning out for Town, he works as a male model all around the world for the likes of Adidas, Marks & Spencer and Timberland, with top agency Select Model Management. When I'm late for training, it might be because I've been refereeing an after-school under-14s match. When Remy turns up half an hour late, it's because his plane back from the photoshoot in Mexico, Barbados or South Africa was delayed a little.

Remy's doing alright but the bottom line in genuinely part-time football is that players make massive sacrifices to be out there on the pitch week after week. For example, as a teacher I'm lucky because I'll have six weeks of summer holidays, but most of my team-mates will be grafting through the summer in their first jobs. When the season ends for them, it's still back to work every Monday morning.

When you dip down into lower leagues, players are literally paying to play, the little they earn being eaten up by travel expenses and loss of their working time and earnings. I think this is where our belief in football being a beautiful game really exists. At the so-called lower levels, players turn out because what gets them up in the morning and brings joy to their lives is the anticipation of doing a day job and then kicking a football around.

The Future of
Non-League Football

ASK ANY club chairman what the toughest part of their job is and most would say paying the bills. For most clubs it's a constant struggle to just keep going – and that was before the pandemic hit. To help them, clubs desperately need more financial trickle-down from the moneybags clubs and organisations at the top of the game.

The Premier League currently hands over £100m a year to non-league grassroots football. In 2019/20 that helped finance 300 new facility projects, 112 grass pitches, 69 artificial pitches and 54 changing rooms. On the face of it, that all looks very impressive. But consider this. During the same period, the Premier League received over £5bn in broadcasting rights from Sky and BT. Add to that the fortunes clubs make from sponsorship, expensive match tickets, matchday hospitality, souvenirs, programmes and replica kits, and they earn an eye-watering amount of money.

In other words, the £100m they give to the grassroots game is only a tiny fraction of what the Premier League rakes in every year. Or expressed differently – one club, Manchester City, spent £100m on one player, Jack Grealish.

He signed a five-year deal on £300,000 a week, so the whole deal will cost Manchester City £172m.

Non-league football needs the big boys to give them more money. Just in terms of self-interest, the Premier League has always benefited from further down the pyramid. Non-league has contributed a steady stream of talented footballers to the top of the game and, for that alone, it deserves investing in. But also, non-league represents the very foundations of our national game.

From a playing point of view, one thing that's long overdue and must be fixed is the state of our pitches. It's a problem that's been a long time in the making and, frankly, is a national disgrace. The FA say we currently lose 150,000 matches each year because of the bloody poor state of our non-league pitches. Not so much a problem in the top National leagues, but the further you go down the pyramid the worse the situation gets. Further down the pyramid, a lot of non-league football pitches are council-run, and because their budgets have been slashed by central government, they in turn have had to cut spending on sports and leisure facilities. But maintaining grass pitches doesn't come cheap, so we return to the debate about artificial pitches, which also aren't cheap. Either way, it's hard to attract young children into the game when the very conditions to play on can often be so dismally poor. At every level of the game, we must make football look more attractive as a participation sport.

Another thought for the future is to consider a winter break and extend the season into the summer months. Again, at non-league level, it's certainly related to problems with pitches. A few weeks of bad weather can play such havoc with the fixture list that often clubs end the regular season trying to play catch-up with their postponed fixtures, often fitting in three matches a week, for weeks on end. That's certainly not good for the players' health and well-being and turns the promotion and relegation battles into a bit of a lottery. For me, I'd advocate a winter break from the Premier League down, pitch problems or not. Germany, France, Italy, Spain, Turkey, Belgium and the Netherlands all have breaks. In Scandinavia, Ukraine and Russia they stop competing for a few months.

Currently, you can only join the Professional Footballers' Association if you play in the Football League. The PFA do a fantastic job on many fronts, but arguably the footballers who need their services the most are in non-league football. I think as well as transforming the National into League Three, any non-league player who's on a professional contract should be welcomed into the PFA. This seems to me a big anomaly. How can you be a full-time footballer earning your living solely from playing the game and not be a professional?

It's time for a reboot between the players and the fans. Clubs should offer Q&As and Zoom chats, to connect with their local communities more. There needs to be more interaction. At my last club, an old and well-established non-league outfit, I was hardly asked to do any community work at all in the three years I was there. One time I helped open the club stall in the market, and on another I went in goal at a primary school fayre and let the kids and their parents pepper me with shots. That's how you get kids wanting to support their local club – by getting out there and making proper connections with them on their turf. Clubs could adopt five or six local schools and offer skills and coaching classes and then perhaps invite entire school teams and their staff along to matches for free, so that they can experience the thrill of a matchday.

Also, if you arranged Zoom chats with players, you could charge a fiver a shot and bring in some income too because, as we know, in non-league, money – or the lack of it – is at the root of everything. The effects of the pandemic only served to point out just how reliant clubs are on their matchday receipts, and they need to start thinking out of the box more to survive.

The further down the pyramid you go, the more the ball is in the air. So, the current debate about heading and whether or not it can lead to dementia is particularly relevant to non-league football. There's a lot of research to support the link and both my grandparents died of dementia, so I know what a brutal illness it can be. Should heading be banned, or somehow reduced? The facts are shocking. There's a lot of research to show that footballers are three and a half times more likely to suffer from dementia than the general population – the figure for defenders is even higher. We've known since the 1920s that repeated blows to the head cause neurological damage and yet the powers that be have done little about it until recently.

The FA has recommended that, pending further research, football clubs limit 'high-force headers' – from a pass over 35 metres away, free kicks, crosses and corners – to no more than ten a week per player. But how will that be policed? Is it to be left up to individual players or placed into a general coaching plan of some kind? What if a player refuses to head a ball in free kick and corner practice because he's already had his ten that week?

Spennymoor recently held a charity friendly against ex-pros from the North-East, such as Craig Hignett and Mark Tinkler, to explore what a match would look like with restrictions on heading the ball. Organised by the Head for Change project, the 'novelty match' had the serious intent of raising public awareness about the issue. For the first half, heading was only allowed in the penalty boxes. In the second, it was outlawed altogether. To begin with players found it hard to adapt and the first foul for a headed ball was given after only two minutes. In the second, with no heading at all, the players had to be ingenious and find different ways of working the ball into the box. The winners, Spennymoor, were awarded the Bill Gates Celebration Cup, named after the former Middlesbrough defender who suffered from dementia, and whose wife, Dr Judith Gates, is behind Head for Change.

I know former England centre-back Terry Butcher, himself no stranger to the headed ball during his illustrious career, has come out and said heading should be banned completely. I'm not sure I'd go that far. I think like most footballers and I can't imagine the game being played without headers. But if more research conclusively proves the link between dementia and heading, are we all putting our future health in real jeopardy? Might there be other routes to explore? Rugby players wear head guards. Could there not be some kind of lightweight guard that could be designed for footballers, to help protect their heads? Or a new design of football that wouldn't have as much impact on the head? Whatever, we'll have to listen to the experts.

From the 2022/23 season, the National League clubs have agreed to a salary cap. It's been reported that in the National League clubs will have a cap of £900,000, while in the National North and South, it'll be £540,000. If clubs are going to survive post-pandemic, wages must be kept at a sustainable level. It's all about survival. But I think an unexpected consequence of this will be that the playing field will level up a little between clubs. Well-managed outfits who spend within their means may yet get more than a sniff at promotion places in the future.

The National League is a total anomaly because it's the only league outside the EFL that's organised on a national basis. It may well be the only so-called non-league in Europe to be so organised. It contains clubs as far north as Halifax, Weymouth to the west, King's Lynn to the east and Dover to the south. More than three-quarters of its clubs are fully professional. Neither fact can be ignored. The National is, in everything but name, a professional nationwide league. So, it's well overdue that it should became League Three and be absorbed into the EFL family. Having personally played in both the National League and League Two, I can say that there's not a lot of difference in standard between the two any longer. This has regularly been shown by the high numbers of National League teams who've beaten League Two opponents in the early rounds of the FA Cup.

The top tier of non-league football has travelled a long way in the last decade. The gap between what used to be the old Conference and League Two was for a long time a gulf, and when a non-league club was promoted into the higher professional division they'd often struggle to survive.

This is no longer the case. Clubs that get into League Two not only expect to stay there, but to thrive. League Two currently has 13 clubs that have come up or bounced back from the National League. In 2021/22, clubs who have been promoted from the National League over the past ten years or so, including Accrington Stanley, AFC Wimbledon, Burton Albion, Cambridge, Cheltenham, Fleetwood Town, Lincoln City, Morecambe Town, Oxford United, Shrewsbury Town and Wycombe Wanderers, have all established themselves in League One. Luton Town are currently playing in the Championship.

The sheer volume of ex-EFL clubs in the National League has helped drive standards up hugely, both on and off the pitch. Not so many years ago, a club that dropped out of League Two would be looking to bounce back immediately. Not anymore. To press, Aldershot, Barnet, Chesterfield, Dagenham & Redbridge, Halifax, Grimsby, Notts County (lest we forget, the world's oldest professional football club), Southend, Stockport, Torquay, Wrexham and Yeovil have all spent years battling it out to get back there. This rise in standards has also sharpened up the ambition of other clubs and, allied to ambitious millionaire businessmen buying into established non-league outfits, it's now become a hugely competitive league. This has all led to a surge in quality and interest.

Gone are the kick and rush days of old. The National leagues contain well-coached, skilful teams who are tactically shrewd and entertaining to watch. Attendances have steadily risen. Wrexham, Stockport, Notts County, Chesterfield and Southend all regularly average bigger crowds than 17 of the current League Two clubs. The profile of the National League has never been higher. Amidst much hullabaloo, Hollywood stars Ryan Reynolds and Rob McElhenney bought out Wrexham FC, with Reynolds promising to make them a global force. BT regularly televises live matches and Non-League Day has become a much-covered annual event.

Some of the bigger National League clubs have recently been paying salaries that have many EFL clubs green with envy. Because of the salary cap, League Two clubs could spend no more than £1m on players' salaries. There's been no such cap in the National League. For example, two players, Danny Rowe and Will Crankshaw, have recently left former Premier League club Bradford City of their own volition because they gained better deals at Chesterfield and Stockport County respectively.

As recently as 2016, a planned revamp of the EFL got a major thumbs-down from the 72 league clubs. The plans proposed adding eight clubs to the 72 and having four divisions of 20 teams. Controversially, the original proposal was to include Premier League B teams – and Celtic and Rangers – as the eight. Nobody much was having any of that, so it was proposed that the extra eight be non-league clubs. Not surprisingly, this dog's breakfast never came to fruition. Part of the EFL's overall plan was to try to cut down on fixtures but, at lower league levels, that would have hit a lot of clubs hard in the pocket, relying as they do on matchday revenue.

For me, the answer would be much simpler. Make the National League into League Three. Three automatic promotions and a play-off spot every season – two relegations into the National Leagues North and South, with the champions of both coming up into the new League Three.

The higher profile of being a Football League club would increase attraction to sponsors and offer more benefits to them from advertising. Clubs would get more media exposure, being in a totally rebranded league, and hopefully more coverage of matches both in live and highlights package form. Yes, agreements would have to be reached over key issues such as the use of artificial pitches, standing not sitting, and alcohol in the grounds. Surely, this isn't beyond the wit of humanity. Football has always been in a state of flux and change, and I believe this is one change that would benefit everyone.

One major spanner in the works for my League Three idea, however, may well be the reality forced upon football by the long-term effects of the Covid pandemic. Although clubs have worked their socks off to stay in business, they're all effectively a season behind in terms of money lost from match revenue. I can only see shorter player contracts, tighter budgets and lower salaries.

Ally that to soaring energy prices, the crises at the petrol pumps and the high cost of travel, and who knows? Perhaps the reverse may well happen, and clubs from League Two and the National League will look at going part-time to save money, and the powers that be will contemplate regionalising both leagues. In other words, have a League Three North and a League Three South – just like in the days of yore. There would be less expensive travel and overnight hotel stays, plus a lot more local derbies.

Appendix 1
TIER 5

National League 2021/22

Club	Ground	Capacity	Founded
Aldershot Town	Recreation Ground	7,100	1992
Altrincham	Moss Lane	7,873	1891
Barnet	The Hive Stadium	6,500	1888
Boreham Wood	Meadow Park	4,500	1948
Bromley	Hayes Lane	5,150	1892
Chesterfield	Technique Stadium	10,600	1866
Dagenham & Redbridge	Victoria Road	6,078	1992
Dover Athletic	Crabble Athletic Ground	5,745	1983
Eastleigh	Silverlake Stadium	5,192	1946
FC Halifax Town	The Shay	14,061	2008
Grimsby Town	Blundell Park	9,031	1878
King's Lynn Town	The Walks	8,200	2010
Maidenhead United	York Road	4,000	1870
Notts County	Meadow Lane	19,841	1862
Solihull Moors	Damson Park	5,500	2007
Southend United	Roots Hall	12,492	1906
Stockport County	Edgeley Park	10,852	1883
Torquay United	Plainmoor	6,200	1899
Wealdstone	Grosvenor Vale	4,085	1899
Weymouth	Bob Lucas Stadium	6,600	1890
Woking	Kingfield Stadium	6,036	1887
Wrexham	Racecourse Ground	10,771	1864
Yeovil Town	Huish Park	9,565	1895

Appendix 2
TIER 6

National League North 2021/22

Club	Ground	Capacity	Founded
AFC Fylde	Mill Farm	6,000	1998
AFC Telford	New Bucks Head	6,380	2004
Alfreton Town	North Street	3,600	1959
Blyth Spartans	Croft Park	4,435	1899
Boston United	Jakeman's Community Stadium	5,000	1933
Brackley Town	St James Park	3,500	1890
Bradford Park Avenue	Horsfall Stadium	3,500	1907
Chester City	Deva Stadium	6,500	2010
Chorley	Victory Park	3,700	1883
Curzon Ashton	Tameside Stadium	3,000	1963
Darlington	Blackwell Meadows*	3,300	2012
Farsley Celtic	The Citadel	4,000	1908
Gateshead	International Stadium	11,800	1977
Gloucester City	New Meadow Park	4,000	1883
Guiseley	Nethermoor Park	4,000	1909
Hereford	Edgar Street	5,213	2014
Kettering Town	Latimer Park**	2,400	1872
Kidderminster Harriers	Aggborough	6,444	1886
Leamington	New Windmill Ground	2,300	1933
Southport	Pure Stadium	6,008	1881
Spennymoor Town	The Brewery Field	4,200	2005
York	York Community Stadium	8,500	1922

* Ground share with Darlington RUFC.
** Ground share with Burton Park Wanderers of Spartan South Midlands League Division 1.

National League South 2021/22

Club	Ground	Capacity	Founded
Bath City	Twerton Park	3,528	1889
Billericay Town	New Lodge	5,000	1880
Braintree Town	Cressing Road	4,222	1898
Chelmsford City	Melbourne Stadium	3,000	1938
Chippenham Town	Hardenhuish Park	3,000	1873
Concord Rangers	Thames Road	3,300	1967
Dartford	Princes Park	4,100	1888
Dorking Wanderers	Meadowbank	3,000	1999
Dulwich Town	Champion Hill	3,000	1893
Eastbourne Borough	Priory Lane	4,151	1964
Ebbsfleet United	Stonebridge Road	4,769	1946
Hampton & Richmond	The Cleo Saul Beveree Stadium	3,500	1921
Havant & Waterlooville	Draper Tools Community Stadium	5,300	1998
Hemel Hempstead Town	Vauxhall Road	3,152	1885
Hungerford Town	Bulpit Lane	3,034	1886
Maidstone United	Gallagher Stadium	4,200	1992
Oxford City	Marsh Lane	3,500	1882
Slough Town	Arbour Park	2,000	1893
St Albans City	Clarence Park	5,007	1908
Tonbridge Angels	Longmead Stadium	3,000	1947
Welling United	Park View Road	4,000	1963

Appendix 3
TIER 7

Northern League Premier 2021/22

Club	Ground	Capacity	Founded
Ashton United	Hurst Cross	4,500	1878
Atherton Collieries	Alder House	2,500	1916
Bamber Bridge	Sir Tom Finney Stadium	3,000	1974
Basford United	Greenwich Avenue	1,600	1900
Buxton	The Silverlands	4,000	1877
FC United of Manchester	Broadhurst Park	4,400	2005
Gainsborough Trinity	The Northolme	4,340	1873
Grantham Town	South Kesteven Sports Stadium	7,500	1874
Hyde United	Ewen Fields	4,250	1919
Lancaster City	Giant Axe	3,513	1911
Matlock Town	Causeway Lane	2,400	1878
Mickleover	Station Road	1,500	1948
Morpeth Town	Craik Park	3,000	1909
Nantwich Town	Weaver Stadium	3,500	1884
Radcliffe	Neuven Stadium	4,000	1949
Scarborough Athletic	Flamingo Land Stadium	2,833	2007
South Shields	Mariners Park	3,000	1974
Stafford Rangers	Marston Road	4,000	1876
Stalybridge Celtic	Bower Fold	6,500	1909
Warrington Town	Cantilever Park	2,550	1949
Whitby Town	Turnbull Ground	3,500	1880
Witton Albion	Wincham Park	4,813	1887

Southern League Premier Central 2021/22

Club	Ground	Capacity	Founded
AFC Rushden & Diamonds	Hayden Road	2,955	2011
Alvechurch	Lye Meadow	3,000	1929
Banbury United	Spencer Stadium	6,500	1931
Barwell	Kirby Road	2,500	1992
Biggleswade Town	Langford Road	3,000	1874
Bromsgrove Sporting	Victoria Ground	3,500	2009
Coalville	Owen Street Sports Ground	2,000	1926
Hednesford Town	Keys Park	6,039	1880
Hitchin Town	Top Field	4,554	1928
Leiston	Victory Road	2,250	1880
Lowestoft Town	Crown Meadow	3,000	1887
Needham Market	Bloomfields	4,000	1919
Nuneaton Borough	Liberty Way	4,614	1889
Peterborough Sports	Lincoln Road	2,300	1908
Redditch United	The Trico Stadium	5,000	1891
Royston Town	Garden Walk	5,000	1875
Rushall Olympic	Dales Lane	1,980	1950
St Ives Town	Westwood Road	2,000	1887
Stourbridge	War Memorial Athletic Ground	2,626	1876
Stratford Town	Knights Lane	1,400	1941
Tamworth	The Lamb Ground	4,963	1933

Southern League Premier South 2021/22

Club	Ground	Capacity	Founded
Beaconsfield Town	Holloways Park	3,500	1994
Chesham United	The Meadow	5,000	1917
Dorchester Town	The Avenue Stadium	5,229	1880
Farnborough	Cherrywood Road	7,000	1967
Gosport Borough	Privett Park	4,500	1944
Hartley Wintney	The Memorial Playing Fields	2,000	1897
Hayes & Yeading United	Skyex Stadium	3,000	2007
Hendon	Silver Jubilee Park	1,990	1908
King's Langley	The Orbital Fasteners Stadium	1,900	1886
Merthyr Town	Penydarren Park	10,000	1909
Metropolitan Police	Imber Court	3,000	1919
Poole Town	Tatnam Ground	2,500	1880
Salisbury	The Raymond McEnhill Stadium	5,000	2015
Swindon Supermarine	The Webbswood Stadium	2,900	1992
Taunton Town	The Cygnet Healthcare Stadium	2,500	1947
Tiverton Town	Ladysmead	3,500	1913
Truro City	Bolitho Park	3,500	1889
Walton Casuals	Elmbridge Sports Hub	2,500	1948
Weston super Mare	The Optima Stadium	3,500	1948
Wimborne Town	Cuthbury	3,250	1878
Yate Town	Lodge Road	2,000	1906

Isthmian League Premier Division 2021/22

Club	Ground	Capacity	Founded
Bishop's Stortford	Woodside Park	4,524	1874
Bognor Regis Town	Nyewood Lane	4,500	1883
Bowers & Pitsea	Len Salmon Stadium	2,661	2003
Brightlingsea Regent	North Road	1,000	2005
Carshalton Athletic	War Memorial Sports Ground	5,000	1905
Cheshunt	Theobald's Lane	3,500	1946
Corinthian Casuals	King George's Field	2,000	1939
Cray Wanderers	Hay Lane	5,000	1860
East Thurrock United	Rookery Hill	3,500	1969
Enfield Town	Queen Elizabeth II Stadium	2,500	2001
Folkestone Invicta	Cheriton Road	4,000	1936
Haringey Borough	Coles Park	2,500	1973
Hornchurch	Hornchurch Stadium	3,500	1923
Horsham	The Camping World Community Stadium	2,000	1881
Kingstonian	King George's Field	2,000	1885
Leatherhead	Fetcham Grove	3,400	1907
Lewes	The Dripping Pan	3,000	1885
Margate	Hartsdown Park	2,100	1896
Merstham	Moatside	2,500	1892
Potter's Bar Town	Parkfield	2,500	1960
Wingate & Finchley	The Maurice Rebak Stadium	1,500	1991
Worthing	Woodside Road	4,000	1886

Appendix 4
TIER 8

Northern League Division One West 2021/22

Club	Ground	Capacity	Founded
1874 Northwich	Townfield	3,000	2012
Bootle	New Bucks Park	3,750	1953
City of Liverpool	Rivacre Park	3,300	2015
Clitheroe	Shawbridge	2,000	1877
Colne	Holt House	1,800	1996
Glossop North End	Surrey Street	1,350	1886
Kendal Town	Parkside Road	2,400	1919
Kidsgrove Athletic	Hollinwood Road	2,000	1952
Leek Town	Harrison Park	3,600	1946
Marine	Rossett Park	3,185	1894
Market Drayton Town	Greenfield Sports Ground	1,000	1969
Mossley	Seel Park	4,500	1903
Newcastle Town	Lyme Valley Stadium	4,000	1964
Prescot Cables	Valerie Park	3,000	1884
Ramsbottom United	Harry Williams Riverside Stadium	2,000	1966
Runcorn Linnets	Millbank Linnets Stadium	1,600	2006
Trafford	Shawe View	1,500	1990
Warrington Rylands 1906	Gorsey Lane	1,345	1906
Widnes	Halton Stadium	13,350	2003
Workington	Borough Park	3,101	1921

Northern League Division One East 2021/22

Club	Ground	Capacity	Founded
Bridlington Town	Queensgate	3,000	1918
Brighouse Town	St Giles Road	1,000	1963
Cleethorpes Town	Linden Club	1,000	1998
Dunston UTS	Wellington Road	2,500	1975
Frickley Athletic	Westfield Lane	2,087	1910
Hebburn Town	Hebburn Town Sports and Social Ground	2,000	1912
Lincoln United	Ashby Avenue	2,714	1938
Liversedge	Clayborn	2,000	1910
Marske United	Mount Pleasant	2,500	1956
Ossett United	Ingfield	1,950	2018
Pickering Town	Mill Lane	2,000	1888
Pontrefact Collieries	Beechnut Lane	1,200	1958
Sheffield	Home of Football Ground	2,089	1857
Shildon	Dean Street	4,700	1890
Stocksbridge Park Metals	Bracken Moor	3,500	1986
Stockton Town	Bishopton Road West	1,800	1979
Tadcaster Albion	Ings Lane	2,000	1892
Worksop Town	Sandy Lane	2,500	1861
Yorkshire Amateur	Bracken Edge	1,550	1918

Northern Premier Division One Midlands 2021/22

Club	Ground	Capacity	Founded
Bedworth United	The Oval	3,000	1895
Belper Town	Christchurch Meadow	2,650	1883
Cambridge City	Bridge Road	4,300	1908
Carlton Town	Bill Stokeld Stadium	1,968	1904
Chasetown	The Scholars Ground	2,000	1954
Coleshill Town	Pack Meadow	2,000	1885
Corby Town	Steel Town	3,893	1948
Daventry Town	Elderstubbs	1,855	1886
Halesowen Town	The Grove	3,150	1873
Histon	Bridge Road	3,800	1904
Ilkeston Town	New Manor Ground	3,029	2017
Loughborough Town	Nanpantan Sports Ground	1,500	1955
Shepshed Dynamo	The Dovecote Stadium	2,500	1994
Soham Town Rangers	Julius Martin Lane	2,000	1947
Spalding United	Sir Halley Stewart Field	3,500	1905
Sporting Khalsa	Noose Lane	Unknown	1990
Stamford	Zeeco Stadium	2,000	1896
Sutton Coldfield Town	Central Ground	2,000	1879
Wisbech Town	Fountain Fresh Park	1,118	1920
Yaxley	Leading Drove	1,000	1962

Southern League Division One Central 2021/22

Club	Ground	Capacity	Founded
AFC Dunstable	Creasey Park	3,200	1981
Aylesbury United	The Meadow	5,000	1897
Barton Rovers	Sharpenhoe Road	4,000	1898
Bedford Town	The Eyrie	3,000	1908
Berkhamsted	Broadwater	2,500	2009
Biggleswade FC	The Eyrie	3,000	2016
Colney Heath	Recreation Ground	1,000	1907
Didcot Town	Loop Meadow Stadium	3,000	1907
FC Romania	Cheshunt Stadium	3,500	2006
Harlow Town	The Harlow Arena	3,500	1879
Hertford Town	Hertingfordbury Park	6,500	1901
Kempston Rovers	Hillgrounds Leisure	2,000	1884
Kidlington	Yarnton Road	1,500	1909
North Leigh	Eynsham Park	2,000	1908
St Neots Town	Rowley Park	3,500	1879
Waltham Abbey	Capershotts	3,000	1944
Wantage Town	Alfredian Park	1,500	1892
Ware	Wodson Park	3,000	1921
Welwyn Garden City	Herns Way	3,000	1921

Southern League Division One South 2021/22

Club	Ground	Capacity	Founded
AFC Totton	Testwood Stadium	3,000	1886
Barnstaple Town	Mill Road	5,000	1904
Bideford AFC	The Sports Ground	6,000	1897
Bristol Manor Farm	The Creek	2,000	1960
Cinderford Town	Causeway Ground	3,500	1922
Cirencester Town	Corinium Stadium	4,500	1889
Evesham United	The Spiers and Hartwell Jubilee Stadium	3,000	1945
Frome Town	Badgers Hill	3,000	1904
Highworth Town	The Elms Recreation Ground	2,000	1893
Larkhall Athletic	Plain Ham	1,000	1914
Lymington Town	The Sports Ground	1,000	1876
Mangotsfield United	Cossham Street	2,500	1951
Melksham Town	Oakfield Stadium	1,000	1876
Paulton Rovers	Athletic Ground	2,500	1881
Plymouth Parkway	Bolitho Park	3,500	1988
Sholing	Mackoy Stadium	1,000	1960
Slimbridge	Thornhill Park	1,500	1902
Willand Rovers	Stan Robinson Ground	1,000	1946
Winchester City	The Simplyhealth City Ground	4,500	1891

Isthmian League South Central Division 2021/22

Club	Ground	Capacity	Founded
Ashford Town	Robert Parker Ground	2,550	1958
Basingstoke Town	Winklebury Sports Complex	2,000	1896
Bedfont Sports	Bedfont Recreation Ground	3,000	2002
Binfield	Hill Farm Lane	1,000	1892
Bracknell Town	Bottom Meadow	1,950	1896
Chalfont St Peter	Mill Meadow	4,500	1926
Chertsey Town	Alwyns Lane	2,500	1890
Chipstead	High Road	2,000	1906
Guernsey	Footes Lane	5,000	2011
Hanwell Town	Powerday Stadium	3,000	1920
Marlow	Alfred Davis Memorial Ground	3,000	1977
Northwood	Acretweed Stadium	3,075	1926
South Park	Whitehall Lane	2,000	1897
Staines Town	Wheatsheaf Park	5,000	1892
Sutton Common Rovers	Gander Green Lane	5,103	1978
Thatcham Town	Waterside Park	1,500	1894
Tooting & Mitcham United	Imperial Fields	3,500	1932
Westfield	Woking Park	1,499	1953
Uxbridge	Honeycroft	3,770	1871

Isthmian League North Central Division 2021/22

Club	Ground	Capacity	Founded
AFC Sudbury	King's Marsh	2,500	1999
Aveley	Park Side	3,500	1927
Barking	Mayesbrook Park	2,500	2006
Basildon United	Gardiners Close	2,000	1963
Brentwood Town	Brentwood Centre Arena	1,000	1954
Bury Town	Ram Meadow	3,000	1872
Canvey Island	Park Lane	4,100	1926
Dereham Town	Aldiss Park	2,500	1884
Felixstowe & Watton United	Dellwood Avenue	2,000	2000
Grays Athletic	Parkside	3,500	1890
Great Wakering Rovers	Burroughs Park	3,000	1919
Hashtag United	Len Salmon Stadium	2,661	2016
Heybridge Swifts	Scraley Road	3,000	1880
Hullbridge Sports	Lower Road	1,500	1945
Maldon & Tiptree	Park Drive	2,800	1946
Romford	Mayesbrook Park	2,500	1876
Stowmarket Town	Greens Meadow	2,500	1883
Tilbury	Chadfields	4,000	1889
Witham Town	The Simarco Stadium	2,500	1876

Isthmian League South East Division 2021/22

Club	Ground	Capacity	Founded
Ashford United	The Homelands	3,200	1891
Burgess Hill Town	Leyland Park	2,500	1882
Chichester City	Oaklands Park	2,000	2000
Corinthian	Gay Dawn Farm	2,000	1972
Cray Valley Paper Mills	Badgers Sports Ground	1,000	1919
East Grinstead Town	East Court	3,000	1890
Faversham Town	Salters Lane	2,000	1884
Hastings United	The Pilot Field	4,050	1893
Haywards Heath Town	Hanbury Park	5,000	1888
Herne Bay	Winches Field	3,000	1886
Lancing	Culver Road	2,000	1941
Phoenix Sports	Phoenix Sports Ground	2,000	1935
Ramsgate	Southwood Stadium	2,500	1945
Sevenoaks Town	Greatness Park	1,150	1883
Sittingbourne	Woodstock Park	3,000	1886
Three Bridges	Jubilee Field	1,500	1901
VCD Athletic	The Oakwood	1,180	1916
Whitehawk	Enclosed Ground	3,126	1945
Whitstable Town	The Belmont Ground	3,000	1886

Appendix 5

TIER 9

Combined Counties League Premier Division North
Combined Counties League Premier Division South
Eastern Counties League Premier Division
Essex Senior Leagues
Hellenic League Premier Division
Midland League Premier Division
North West Counties League Premier Division
Northern Counties East League Premier Division
Northern League Division One
Southern Combination League Premier Division
Southern Counties East League Premier Division
Spartan South Midlands League Premier Division
United Counties League Premier Division North
United Counties League Premier Division South
Wessex League Premier Division
Western League Premier Division

TIER 10

Combined Counties League Division One
Eastern Counties League Division One North
Eastern Counties League Division One South
Hellenic League Division One

Midland League Division One
North West Counties League Division One North
North West Counties League Division One South
Northern Counties East League Division One
Northern League Division Two
South West Peninsula League Premier East
South West Peninsula League Premier West
Southern Combination League Division One
Southern Counties East League Division One
Spartan South Midlands League Division One
United Counties League Division One
Wessex League Division One
Western League Division One

TIER 11

Regional Feeder Leagues
Anglian Combination Premier Division
Bedfordshire County League Premier Division
Cambridgeshire County League Premier Division
Central Midlands League Premier Division North
Central Midlands League Premier Division South
Cheshire League Premier Division
Devon Football League North & East Division
Devon Football League South & West Division
Dorset Premier League
Essex & Suffolk Border League Premier Division
Essex Olympian League Premier Division
Gloucestershire County League
Hampshire Premier League Senior Division
Hampshire Premier League Senior Division
Hertfordshire Senior County League Premier Division

Humber Premier League Premier Division
Kent County League Premier Division
Leicestershire Senior League Premier Division
Lincolnshire League
Liverpool Premier League Premier Division
Manchester League Premier Division
Mid-Sussex League Premier Division
Middlesex County League Premier Division
Midland League Division Two
Northamptonshire Combination League Premier Division
Northern Alliance Premier Division
North Riding League Premier Division
Nottinghamshire Senior League Premier Division
Oxfordshire Senior League Premier Division
Peterborough & District League Premier Division
Salop Leisure Football League Premier Division
Sheffield & Hallamshire County Premier
Somerset County League Premier
Southern Combination League Division Two
Spartan South Midlands League Division Two
St Piran League East Division
St Piran League West Division
Staffordshire County Senior League Premier Division
Suffolk & Ipswich League Senior Division
Surrey Elite Intermediate League
Thames Valley Premier League Premier Division
Wearside League Division One
West Cheshire League Division One
West Lancashire League Premier
West Midlands (Regional) League
West Yorkshire League Premier Division

Wiltshire Senior League
York League Premier Division
Yorkshire Amateur League Supreme Division

TIER 12 – 61 Leagues

TIER 13 – 63 Leagues

TIER 14 – 74 Leagues

TIER 15 – 68 Leagues

TIER 16 – 55 Leagues

TIER 17 – 35 Leagues

TIER 18 – 17 Leagues

TIER 19 – 8 Leagues

TIER 20 – 2 Leagues

TIER 21 – 1 League. Quite literally in a league of its own, the Central and South Norfolk League Division Five.

Index

N
Nepal 223
Newport County 65
Newtown 33
Non-League Day 125, 246
Non-League Football
Show 194
Non-League Paper 193–
194
North Ferriby 64, 88, 124
Norwood, James 221
Notts County 96, 99, 129,
246
Nuneaton Borough 32

O
Okenabirhie, Fejir 221
Olutade, Ibrahim 222
Oxford United 65, 245

P
Paine, Alex 222
Parker, Mitchell 222
Pearson, Matty 221
Panther, Emmanuel 61
Peterborough United 24
Phillips, Kevin 67
Professional Footballers
Association (PFA) 15,
152, 169–170, 242
Pukki, Teemu 154
Purkiss, Ben 61

R
Real Sociedad 56
Reynolds, Ryan 99–100,
180, 246

Rhyl 33, 230
Robinson, Paul 20
Rollins, Jay 199
Ross County 214
Rowe, Danny 58, 246
Rushden & Diamonds 65,
199

S
St Albans 32, 65, 221
St George's 169–170
St Ives 112
Salford City 30, 179, 220
Sankaran, Chann 206
Scarborough 31, 76, 91, 129
Scholes, Paul 17, 70–71, 182
Shackleton, Len 174
Shakespeare, Craig 67
Sheffield FC 29
Sheffield Wednesday 66,
202
Shrewsbury Town 245
Slovakia 219
Smalling, Chris 66
Southampton FC 59–60,
66, 78
Southend United 96
Southport FC 31, 96, 114
Spennymoor Town 243–
244
Stafford Rangers 32
Stainton, Nathan 59
Stalybridge Celtic 98
Sterling, Raheem 36, 160
Stockport County 31, 63,
96, 99, 128, 164, 180, 227,
247